This Book may be kept

FOURTEEN DAYS

A fine of TWO CENTS will be charged for each day
the Book is kept over time.

Mar 14 '59			
Mar 31 '59			
Feb 12 '60			
Feb 26 '60			
May 25 '60			
May 7 '64			
May 26 '64			
May 8 '65			
Apr 28 '66			
Feb 1 '69			
Mar 12 '69			
Mar 27 '69			
Jun 24 70			
Jan 27 '71			
Mar 16 '71			
Mar 10 '75			

DEVELOPING SPELLING POWER

By KARLENE V. RUSSELL

Coordinator of Language Arts
Vermont State Department of Education

HELEN A. MURPHY

Professor of Education
Boston University

and DONALD D. DURRELL

Professor of Education
Boston University

WORLD BOOK COMPANY · YONKERS-ON-HUDSON, NEW YORK

372.42
R91d

TABLE OF CONTENTS

35,913
Jan. 1958

Lessons		*Pages*
1–4	INITIAL CONSONANTS	1
5–6	FINAL CONSONANTS	20
7–8	INITIAL BLENDS	29
9–10	FINAL BLENDS	45
11	VOWELS: LONG AND SHORT SOUNDS	59
12–20	WORD STRUCTURE: COMPOUND WORDS, SYLLABICATION, PREFIXES AND SUFFIXES	63
21	REVIEW	92
22	LETTERS WITHIN WORDS	95
23–25	WORDBUILDING	99
26–29	USE OF DICTIONARY: SYLLABICATION AND ACCENT; SPELLING	111
30	WORD ANALYSIS	128

FOREWORD

IT HAS LONG BEEN CLEAR that children of equal intelligence may differ widely in ability to spell. Research has revealed the fact that visual perception and auditory perception, which are important factors in the development of reading ability, are also important factors in learning to spell. Another outcome of research is the finding that these perceptual abilities respond readily to teaching.

The lessons of *Developing Spelling Power* are designed to develop, at the intermediate grade level, these auditory and visual discrimination abilities that have been demonstrated to be so important in spelling and other aspects of language learning. They are directed at strengthening the pupils' powers of listening and of observation, at sharpening their acuity in word perception. They are not designed to teach a specific spelling vocabulary; but the words used to exemplify particular word elements were chosen largely from generally accepted spelling vocabularies for Grades Four, Five, and Six. Some additional words have been included from the vocabularies likely to be encountered in classroom activities such as units of study on health, safety, or the community.

Experimental Background

The materials of *Developing Spelling Power* were developed experimentally by the authors. The final series of lessons were tried out with an experimental group of 600 children in intermediate grades (200 from each of the Grades Four to Six), while another control group of 600 in the same communities, matched for spelling ability and intelligence, continued with their customary spelling instruction. The tryout continued for three months, during which time the lessons of *Developing Spelling Power* were used with the experimental group three days a week, while two days were given to the regular spelling instruction. At the end of the three months, it was found that the control group had made slightly less than the normal gain in spelling ability to be expected during the three months' period. On the other hand, the fourth-grade pupils who were given the lessons of *Developing Spelling Power* had gained ten months in spelling ability and the fifth- and sixth-grade pupils had gained six months. The children whose spelling ability was initially below fourth-grade level made the greatest gains. All measurements of growth were determined by the Stanford Achievement Intermediate Grade Spelling Test.

Three months after the experimental tryout had been concluded, supplementary measures showed that the pupils in the experimental groups were able to spell more words that had been taught than could the pupils who were taught exclusively by the conventional method. Also, the pupils using *Developing Spelling Power* made markedly superior scores on the Gates Word Pronunciation Test VII.

Fitting the Lessons to the School Program

In usual situations where a grade list of spelling words and study plan are prescribed, as in a spelling textbook, *Developing Spelling Power* may be used in several ways: (*1*) on one or two days of the week, lessons from this book may be used in lieu of the lessons of the customary weekly instructional plan in spelling; (*2*) without affecting the usual weekly plan of spelling lessons, several lessons from this book may be used at other available times during the week — perhaps during a language or reading period, since the development of auditory and visual discrimination is an aid both to word recognition and to vocabulary building as well as to spelling; (3) with classes revealing marked spelling disability, the thirty lessons of this book may be used exclusively for six or more weeks, during the early part of the year, and the prescribed list and study plan taken up later; (4) with a group of slow learners within a class, the lessons may be administered at periods apart from the regular daily spelling lesson.

Teachers developing spelling lists from "Units" taught may use these materials to insure no loss of underlying word-building skills and thus feel more secure in curriculum experimentation.

The English language arts are so closely interwoven that *Developing Spelling Power* will be useful to remedial reading teachers and in clinics. Though designed for the middle grades, it has been used to advantage for special work at the junior high school level.

Presentation of Lessons

Each lesson of this book offers text material of two kinds: directions and suggestions to the teacher and materials to be read or spoken to the pupil. Directions to the teacher are enclosed in brackets and are printed in smaller type. (An examination of Lesson 1 will acquaint the teacher with the two types of material.) A preliminary study of each lesson will enable the teacher to conduct the lesson with more spontaneity (and consequently better results) than will a reading of material unfamiliar to her.

Twenty minutes is the normal time allotment for a lesson. However, since close attention on the part of the class or group is a first essential of a successful lesson, it is advisable to discontinue a lesson at a suitable stopping point if attention appears to lag, and to complete the lesson at a later period.

Clear enunciation by the teacher is essential to the development of auditory discrimination on the part of pupils. However, in an exercise in which pupils are asked to identify a word or words that differ auditorially from the other words in the dictated list, the teacher should not, by stress or emphasis of the differing sound, furnish a cue to the words to be identified.

Letter sounds should not be given in isolation by either teacher or pupil; that is, *letters are to be identified by name, not by sound.* Though the pupil hears and identifies the *sound* of the letter *s* at the beginning of a word, he should name that sound as the letter *s*, not as *"s-s-s."*

In connection with most lessons, written responses are called for. The writing is sometimes done by the pupils on ordinary paper, but at other times the written exercises require specially prepared Worksheets. These Worksheets, of which there are sixteen, are bound in a separate booklet for use by the pupils for certain specified lessons. The Worksheets serve both as an extension of the learning practice and as a kind of test that will reveal the pupils' grasp of the learnings. Each pupil should have a copy of the Worksheet booklet.

All written exercises should be checked under the direction of the teacher. In general, it is desirable for the teacher to inspect all written work as closely as possible from time to time in order to make certain of the correctness of the check by the pupils.

When pupils reveal difficulties in performing the exercises in any lesson, the lesson should be repeated at a later period.

ACKNOWLEDGMENTS

THE WRITERS WISH TO EXPRESS their gratitude to the superintendents of schools in Vermont for permission to conduct the study in their schools; to the teachers who cooperated in the program; and to members of the Boston University Educational Clinic who did individual testing.

INITIAL CONSONANTS:

f, b, h, g, c

AUDITORY IDENTIFICATION

[See that each child has paper and pencil ready. Exercise 1 is a preparatory lesson, designed to check the child's ability to write the letters of the alphabet as well as to recognize their sounds. It includes all the letters except *x*.

As you dictate, speak each word distinctly, but be careful not to overemphasize the sound of the initial letter. When you refer to a letter, say its name, not its sound. Direct each exercise as suggested.]

1. I am going to say a word. Listen to the sound of its first letter. Then write the first letter of the word after I say it.

Listen to this word: *family.* [Pause while children write the initial letter.] What letter did you write? Yes, *family* begins with *f.* [Write "1. f" on the board.]

Listen again and write the first letter of this word: *beast.* [Pause.] What letter did you write? Yes, *b* is right. [Write "2. b" on the board.]

Listen: *every.* [Pause.] How many wrote *e?* [Write "3. e" on the board.]

Now you will work alone. Write the numbers 4 to 25 in one or two columns on your papers. [Pause.]

1

Write the *first* letter of each word that I say. [Dictate the following words with their numbers.]

4. gain	9. over	13. dance	17. sing	21. rice
5. horse	10. lace	14. yes	18. quick	22. jail
6. violet	11. zoo	15. kettle	19. able	23. pipe
7. cabbage	12. wing	16. machine	20. table	24. next
8. icicle				25. useful

[At the close, write each number and the correct initial letter on the board, as "4. g." Say the number and the letter and have the children check their responses.]

2. Now we shall try something a little different. Listen. [Dictate.]

factory   four   fault   feather

With what letter does each word begin? Yes, each word begins with *f*. [Write *f* on the board.] I am going to say some other words. Some of them begin with *f*, and some do not begin with *f*. Write the first letter of each word that *does not* begin with *f*. Listen carefully. Ready! [Dictate.]

famous   follow   farther   garage   fasten

February   cage   farming   fearful   harm

What letters did you write? Did you write *c*, *g*, and *h*? [Write the letters on the board.] *Cage* begins with *c*. [Point to *c*.] *Garage* begins with *g*. [Point.] *Harm* begins with *h*. [Point to *h*.] All the other words begin with *f*. [Repeat the words if many pupils failed to give the correct response.]

3. Listen:

band   bird   beet   board

What is the first letter of each of these words? Yes, each word begins with *b*. [Write *b* on the board.] Now I am going to say some other words. Some begin with *b*, and some do not begin with *b*. Write the first letter of each word that *does not* begin with *b*. Listen carefully. Ready!

bake	catch	balloon	behave	banjo
gas	butter	forget	hurry	bite

Did you write *g, c, f,* and *h?* [Write the letters on the board. Point to each as you say the following words.] *Gas* begins with *g*. *Catch* begins with *c*. *Forget* begins with *f*. *Hurry* begins with *h*. The other words begin with *b*.

4. Listen:

> haven't   home   hidden   habit

What is the first letter of each of these words? Yes, each word begins with *h*. [Write *h* on the board.] Now listen carefully and write the first letter of each word that *does not* begin with *h*. [Dictate.]

hall	ham	heavy	biscuit	hero
forest	hurt	heat	hatchet	hope

What letters did you write? Yes, *f* and *b* are right. [Write these letters on the board.] *Forest* begins with *f*. [Point.] *Biscuit* begins with *b*. [Point.] All the other words begin with *h*.

5. Listen to these words:

> gift   goose   gown   gather

With what letter does each of these words begin? Yes, each of these words begins with *g*. [Write *g* on the board.] Now I am going to say some more words. Listen carefully. Write the first letter of each word that *does not* begin with *g*. [Dictate.]

| golden | basket | gasoline | hail | gain |
| follow | gallon | giving | gift | guppy |

What letters did you write? *F*, *b*, and *h* are correct. [Write these letters on the board. Point to them as suggested in previous exercises.] *Follow* begins with *f*. *Basket* begins with *b*. *Hail* begins with *h*. All the others begin with *g*. Listen to all the words again. [Repeat the ten words.]

6. Listen:

> canoe   copy   cane   cook

What is the first letter in each of these words? Yes, the letter *c*. [Write *c* on the board.]

I am going to say other words. Some begin with *c*, and some do not begin with *c*. Listen carefully.

Write the first letter of each word that *does not* begin with *c*.

| calf | concert | curl | fairly | cushion |
| core | bicycle | camp | gulf | curtain |

How many wrote *b*, *f*, and *g*? [Write the letters on the board.] *Bicycle* begins with *b*. [Point to *b*.] *Fairly* begins with *f*. *Gulf* begins with *g*. All the other words begin with the letter *c*.

VISUAL IDENTIFICATION

[Each child should have his Worksheet booklet before him, opened to Worksheet 1. Call attention to the two exercises, explaining that exercise 1 is for Lesson 1, and that it is to be used today. Read the direction for this exercise with the group. Then proceed as follows.]

Look at the fifteen rows of words in this exercise. See the word *Sample* before rows 1 and 2.

Look at the words in row 1 as I read them aloud. [Read the words below distinctly.]

(Sample) 1. bacon   cottage   fair   gain   height

I will write one of these words on the board. Look at it closely before I erase it. Then you are to find that word in row 1 and draw a circle around it. Ready! Begin!

[Write "1. bacon" on the board and point to it while you silently count to five. Then erase it, and wait for the children to find and circle the word.]

Which word did you circle? The first word, *bacon*, is correct. The first letter in *bacon* is *b*.

Now look at the words in sample row 2 on your paper as I read them.

(Sample) 2. cabin   garage   history   book   <u>fallen</u>

I will write one of the words in row 2. Look at it closely before I erase it. [Write "2. fallen" on the board. Count five to yourself before erasing.] Circle the word in row 2 that is the same as the one I wrote. [Pause.] How many circled the last word in the row? *Fallen* is correct. *Fallen* begins with *f*.

Now you will work alone. I will write the row number and a word. Then I will erase it. Look carefully at each word in that row and circle the word that is the same as the one I wrote. [The remaining rows follow on page 6.]

[Write each row number and the underlined word. Count to five and erase the word. *Do not say the word.* Begin with row 3 and end with row 15.

3. garden	before	<u>figure</u>	higher	cage
4. giggle	<u>hunter</u>	could	funny	bundle
5. high	<u>biscuit</u>	gallop	concert	football
6. <u>golden</u>	final	curl	hearth	bitter
7. family	butter	<u>camping</u>	gingham	heavy
8. collect	hidden	<u>goose</u>	feeling	beware
9. gasoline	farmer	hedge	<u>captain</u>	border
10. <u>beast</u>	cape	bunny	hinder	girl
11. howl	<u>build</u>	gable	follow	casting
12. fender	guard	hundred	<u>coffee</u>	balloon
13. <u>hammer</u>	bicycle	father	gallon	curtain
14. gorge	candle	bother	carpet	<u>forget</u>
15. fifteen	<u>hungry</u>	guide	coach	beaver

At the close of this exercise, read the correct word for each row and ask the children to check their responses.]

WRITING FROM VISUAL MEMORY

[Direct the children to exercise 2 on Worksheet 1.]

Now you will find out whether you can write words from memory. I will write a row number and a word on the board. Study it carefully for five seconds. Then I will erase the word. Write it on the right line in exercise 2. Ready. [Be sure to have the attention of the children as you write each word.]

1. fasten	3. hunter	5. canoe	7. copy	9. banana
2. board	4. guess	6. garage	8. follow	10. harm

[When the children have finished, spell the words so that they may correct their responses. Do not have the worksheet detached as exercises 3 and 4 on the reverse side will be used in connection with Lesson 2.

Lesson 2

INITIAL CONSONANTS:

l, m, d, j, k, n, p, q

AUDITORY IDENTIFICATION

[The exercises in this lesson follow the procedure used in Lesson 1. Each child should have paper and pencil. Speak each dictated word very distinctly. When you name the list of words that includes some having different initial consonants, speak distinctly but do not overstress the initial consonants. When you refer to letters, give their names, not their sounds.]

1. Listen to these words:

     lawn   lamp   leaf

With what letter does each word begin? Yes, each one begins with *l*. [Write *l* on the board.] Now listen carefully to the words I shall name. [Dictate slowly enough to allow time for children to write the letters.] Write the first letter of each word that *does not* begin with *l*.

     long   beach   hang   lantern   lap   largest
     laugh   laundry   lunch   little   cane   labor

What letters did you write? *B*, *h*, and *c* are right. [Write these letters on the board.] *Beach* begins with *b*. [Point to *b*.] *Hang* begins with *h*. [Point.] *Cane* begins with *c*. [Point.]

2. Listen:

material money melt

With what letter does each word begin? Each one begins with *m*. [Write *m* on the board.] Now listen carefully to each of the following words. Write the first letter of each word that *does not* begin with *m*.

music given maple market match mile

meeting beauty catch motor listen milk

What letters did you write? *G*, *b*, *c*, and *l* are right. *Given* begins with *g*. *Beauty* begins with *b*. *Catch* begins with *c*. *Listen* begins with *l*. [Write each letter on the board and point to it as directed in earlier exercises.]

3. Listen:

deer daisy dentist

With what letter does each word begin? Each one begins with *d*. [Write *d* on the board.] Now listen carefully. Write the first letter of each of the following words that *does not* begin with *d*.

daughter daylight desk lion December

decorate dollar dish deep middle

What letters did you write? *L* and *m* are right. [Write *l* and *m* on the board.]

Lion begins with *l*, [Point.] and *middle* begins with *m*. [Point.]

4. Listen:

jolly   joke   June

With what letter does each word begin? Each one begins with *j*. [Write *j* on the board.]

Now listen carefully. I will say some more words. Write the first letter of each of the following words that *does not* begin with *j*.

jaw	jelly	jewels	mine	date	job
join	joke	field	jolly	living	juice

What letters did you write? *F*, *m*, *d*, and *l* are right. [Write these letters on the board.] *Field* begins with *f*. [Point.] *Mine* begins with *m*. *Date* begins with *d*. *Living* begins with *l*.

5. Listen:

kinds   keen   kill

With what letter does each word begin? Each one begins with *k*. [Write *k* on the board.] Now listen carefully to each word that I say. Write the first letter of each word that *does not* begin with *k*.

key	kick	kettle	maple	kernel
king	kindly	dozen	label	jewel

What letters did you write? *D*, *m*, *l*, and *j* are right. [Write these letters on the board.] *Dozen* begins with *d*. *Maple* begins with *m*. *Label* begins with *l*. *Jewel* begins with *j*. [Point to each letter.]

6. Listen:

needle   nature   neck

With what letter does each word begin? Each word begins with *n*. [Write *n* on the board.] Listen carefully to each word I say. Write the first letter of each word that *does not* begin with *n*.

nature	nearer	king	naughty	neighbor
neck	jungle	neatly	needle	November

What letters did you write? *J* and *k* are right. [Write *j* and *k* on the board.] *Jungle* begins with *j* and *king* begins with *k*. [Point to the letters.]

7. Listen to these words:

pencil   pine   pair

With what letter does each word begin? Each one begins with *p*. [Write *p* on the board.] I will say some more words. Listen carefully. Write the first letter of each word that *does not* begin with *p*.

page	pumpkin	join	pitch	dipper
pail	person	pillow	kept	palace

What letters did you write? *J, k,* and *d* are right. [Write the letters on the board.] *Join* begins with *j.* [Point.] *Kept* begins with *k. Dipper* begins with *d.*

8. Listen:

quilt   quick   quart

With what letter does each word begin? Each one begins with *q*. [Write the words on the board.] What letter follows *q* in each word? Listen carefully to the words I will say. Write the first letter of each word that *does not* begin with *q*.

queen	peel	quill	queer	question	quarter
quiet	never	quit	palace	kitchen	quarrel

What did you write? *P*, *n*, *p*, and *k* are right. [Write these letters on the board.] *Peel* and *palace* begin with *p*. *Never* begins with *n*. *Kitchen* begins with *k*.

VISUAL IDENTIFICATION

[Each child should have Worksheet 1 before him.]

Today you will do exercise 3 of Worksheet 1. Turn your worksheet over and find exercise 3. I will write one of the words in row 1. Study it closely. After I erase it, circle the word in row 1 that is the same as the one I wrote. [Write "1. lamb," but do not pronounce the word. Count to five silently and then erase the word.]

1. farming   <u>lamb</u>   deep   geese   haul

Which word did you circle? The word *lamb* is right.

[Proceed with rows 2–9 as directed for row 1: write the row number, the underlined word in that row, and count five silently before erasing it; then direct the pupils to circle the word in the row that is the same as the word you wrote.

2. fasten	canoe	hall	<u>jar</u>	lace
3. maid	ham	jam	lad	<u>nail</u>
4. banner	gifts	field	<u>quiet</u>	laundry
5. handle	feather	girl	joke	<u>leap</u>
6. job	<u>mask</u>	hate	jewels	laugh
7. <u>ditch</u>	lap	jest	march	join
8. jelly	hatch	largest	<u>key</u>	market
9. laugh	money	<u>people</u>	queer	jolly

At the close of the exercise, read the correct word (underlined) for each row so that the children may check their responses.]

WRITING FROM VISUAL MEMORY

[Exercise 4 on Worksheet 1 calls upon the child to visualize a written word and then write it from memory.]

Look at exercise 4 on the back of Worksheet 1. I will write a word on the board. Look at it carefully for five seconds. When I erase the word, write it on the line after the right number. Ready. Watch! [Write each word and its number. Be sure to say each word distinctly before you erase it.]

1. page	3. quick	5. market	7. quiet	9. note
2. laugh	4. polite	6. jelly	8. dance	10. kindly

[At the close, spell each word so that the children may correct their responses.]

Lesson **3** | ## INITIAL CONSONANTS:
r, s, t, v, w, y, z

AUDITORY IDENTIFICATION

[Each child should have paper and pencil ready. Proceed as in Lessons 1 and 2.]

1. Listen:

raft   rice   ranch   ribbon

With what letter does each word begin? Each one begins with *r*. [Write *r* on the board.] Listen carefully to some other words that I will say. Write the first letter of each word that *does not* begin with *r*.

rail	baker	rainbow	roar	return
rubber	reindeer	careful	date	rooster

What letters did you write? *B, c,* and *d* are right. [Write the letters on the board.] *Baker* begins with *b*. [Point.] *Careful* begins with *c*. [Point.] *Date* begins with *d*.

2. Listen:

same	sentence	south	several

With what letter does each word begin? Each one begins with *s*. [Write *s* on the board.] Write the first letter of each word that *does not* begin with *s*.

safety	surprise	sail	gather	soup
second	family	salt	habit	soft

What letters did you write? *F, g,* and *h* are right. [Write the letters on the board.] *Family* begins with *f*. [Point to *f*.] *Gather* begins with *g*. *Habit* begins with *h*.

3. Listen:

taken	table	tulip	taste

With what letter does each word begin? Each one begins with *t*. [Write *t* on the board.] Listen carefully to the words I will say. Write the first letter of each word that *does not* begin with *t*.

taught	tumble	juice	toast	leader
tiger	tank	tap	kindly	team

What letters did you write? *J*, *k*, and *l* are right. [Write these letters on the board.] *Juice* begins with *j*. [Point.] *Kindly* begins with *k*. *Leader* begins with *l*.

4. Listen:

> valentine   violin   view   vine

With what letter does each word begin? Each one begins with *v*. [Write *v*.] Listen carefully. Write the first letter of each word that *does not* begin with *v*.

> vacation   mouth   violet   valley   victory
> vegetable   vine   neat   visit   village

What letters did you write? *M* and *n* are right. [Write the letters on the board.] *Mouth* begins with *m*. [Point.] *Neat* begins with *n*. [Point.]

5. Listen:

> washing   windy   world   wise

With what letter does each word begin? Each one begins with *w*. [Write *w* on the board.] Listen carefully and write the first letter of each of the following words that *does not* begin with *w*.

> walnut   pile   waited   wonder   repeat
> waiting   wear   question   windmill   wasn't

What letters did you write? *P*, *q*, and *r* are right. [Write these letters.] *Pile* begins with *p*. [Point.] *Question* begins with *q*. [Point.] *Repeat* begins with *r*.

6. Listen:

> yarn   yell   yesterday   young

With what letter does each word begin? Yes, each one begins with *y*. [Write *y* on the board.] Now listen carefully to the words I will say. Write the first letter of each word that *does not* begin with *y*.

| year | yard | tablet | yourself | yet |
| yes | sunny | yellow | visitor | yours |

What letters did you write? *S*, *t*, and *v* are right. [Write *s*, *t*, and *v* on the board.] *Sunny* begins with *s*. [Point to *s*.] *Tablet* begins with *t*. [Point to *t*.] *Visitor* begins with *v*. [Point.]

7. Listen:

zoo   zero   zone   zebra

With what letter does each of these words begin? Yes, each of the words begins with *z*. [Write *z* on the board.] Now listen to some other words I will say. Write the first letter of each word that *does not* begin with *z*.

| zinc | zipper | zinnia | zoom |
| wipe | zigzag | yarn | juice |

What letters did you write? *W*, *y*, and *j* are right. [Write the letters.] *Wipe* begins with *w*. [Point.] *Yarn* begins with *y*. *Juice* begins with *j*.

VISUAL IDENTIFICATION

[The children should have Worksheet 2 before them.]

1. This is like the first worksheet you had. Find exercise 1 on Worksheet 2. I am going to write one of the words in row 1 on the board. Look at it closely. Then I will erase it very quickly. You are to find the word in row 1 on your

worksheet and draw a circle around it. [Write "1. zero."
Then erase after you silently count five.]

1. keen   nail   pack   <u>zero</u>   race

Which word did you circle? The fourth word, *zero*, is
right. With what letter does *zero* begin?

[If a second sample is needed, handle row 2 as suggested for
row 1, using the word *young*. Then explain.]

Now you will work alone. Begin with row 3 (or 2).
I will write a row number and a word and then erase it.
You will study the word, find the word in that row on your
worksheet, and draw a circle around it.

[Rows 2–10 are here reproduced, with the key word for each
row underlined. Proceed with these other rows as suggested for
row 1.

2. named	kept	quart	radio	<u>young</u>
3. nap	paddle	quarter	<u>raft</u>	saddle
4. <u>sack</u>	vacation	tablet	wade	paid
5. sad	poem	<u>tacks</u>	valentine	walnut
6. <u>valley</u>	wait	tag	naughty	village
7. view	rainy	<u>waiting</u>	safety	tale
8. page	song	<u>zone</u>	pear	pail
9. <u>quick</u>	kettle	key	quiet	kick
10. wash	weary	vain	<u>wagon</u>	wear

After the completion of the exercise, direct a check of the
children's work by naming the correct word in each row.]

2.   [Direct the group to look at exercise 2 on their worksheet.
Read the directions with them. Then proceed to write the following words on the board, as follows: "1. raise." Erase after you

have counted to five silently. Then pause while the children write. Here are the words:

1. raise   3. taste   5. watch   7. zone   9. world
2. second   4. visit   6. yarn   8. tired   10. young

At the close of the exercise, direct a check. Spell each word and have the children check their spelling.]

Lesson **4** | # INITIAL CONSONANTS:
REVIEW

[This lesson, based on Worksheet 3, checks the pupils' knowledge of the initial consonants presented in Lessons 1–3. Before attempting to take up Lesson 4, examine Worksheet 3 to acquaint yourself with the arrangement and purpose of the exercises. Also, read through the following directions for the presentation of the exercises before attempting to give them to the pupils.

See that each pupil has Worksheet 3 before him. Call the children's attention to exercise 1 and have them note the 20 rows of letters. Read the direction with the group.]

AUDITORY IDENTIFICATION

1.   Look at row 1 in exercise 1. Do you see the five letters in that row? I am going to say a word. Think of the first letter in the word I say. Find that letter in row 1 and draw

a circle around it. Now listen: row 1 — *family*. Find the first letter of *family* in row 1 and draw a circle around it. [Pause.] What letter did you circle? Yes, *f* is the right letter. *Family* begins with *f*.

[Here are the words to be dictated. After each word are the letters that appear on the worksheet. If the pupils need further demonstration of what they are to do, use 2 and 3 as samples. Direct a check after each five exercises. The underlined letters are those that the pupils should circle.]

2. boot	d	f	<u>b</u>	p	q	11. nail	m	<u>n</u>	p	r	s
3. hole	<u>h</u>	l	m	n	f	12. pound	q	r	d	<u>p</u>	v
4. guess	p	<u>g</u>	l	h	r	13. quart	p	f	<u>q</u>	b	h
5. curtain	f	b	h	g	<u>c</u>	14. rice	b	s	t	<u>r</u>	c
						15. sack	<u>s</u>	r	v	m	n
6. low	h	d	f	<u>l</u>	t	16. tag	<u>t</u>	r	s	d	h
7. machine	n	w	v	d	<u>m</u>	17. vacation	<u>v</u>	w	m	s	t
8. depart	p	q	c	<u>d</u>	b	18. wagon	v	n	m	<u>w</u>	h
9. jail	r	b	h	<u>j</u>	k	19. yell	m	d	t	<u>y</u>	r
10. keen	h	<u>k</u>	b	g	p	20. zoo	b	h	p	q	<u>z</u>

[Check the completed worksheets to discover with which initial consonants individual children are having difficulty.]

VISUAL IDENTIFICATION

Now you are going to use exercise 2 on the other side of Worksheet 3. Read the direction at the top.

Look at sample row 1 and notice the four words. [See sample rows 1, 2, and 3 on page 19 opposite.] I will write one of those words. Watch closely as I write the word. Then I will erase it. [Write the underlined word with its number: "1. raft." Erase it after counting five silently.] Find that same word in sample row 1 and draw a circle around it.

[After the children have circled the word, proceed to check as follows.] Which word did you circle? The second word, *raft*, is the right one.

[Proceed with Samples 2 and 3, using the underlined word in each sample below. Follow each with the check suggested above.

(Sample) 1. pain	<u>raft</u>	wait	soft	
(Sample) 2. paddle	quarter	<u>camel</u>	angel	
(Sample) 3. naughty	waited	paid	tablet	<u>kettle</u>

Proceed with rows 4–12. Follow the procedure suggested above in connection with the samples. The nine rows of words follow. At the end of the lesson, direct a check of the children's responses, using questions as suggested in connection with the sample exercises. Have children name the words they circled.

4. year	question	kill	<u>wagon</u>	
5. tack	<u>pail</u>	sad	wind	kept
6. valley	<u>quick</u>	tag	naughty	key
7. <u>zone</u>	vine	tan	save	zero
8. feather	mask	joke	<u>lazy</u>	handle
9. job	field	<u>jelly</u>	laundry	juicy
10. navy	maple	match	<u>nature</u>	needle
11. <u>barrel</u>	daylight	bank	band	barber
12. windy	verse	spot	riddle	<u>toast</u>]

GENERAL CHECK

[After the worksheet exercises have been completed and checked, conduct a "Listening Bee." Select words from Worksheets 2 and 3. Ask each contestant to name the first letter of a word you say. Pronounce each word distinctly.]

Lesson 5 | **FINAL CONSONANTS:**
n, f, s, r, m, d, l, t

AUDITORY IDENTIFICATION

[Each child should have paper and pencil ready. With this lesson there is a shift from *initial consonants*, with which Lessons 1–4 were concerned, to *final consonants* of words. Proceed as suggested below.]

Up to now, you have been talking and learning about letters that *begin* words that you speak and write. In this lesson, you will be listening to and thinking about some letters that *end* many words.

I am going to say some words that end differently. Listen closely for the last letter of this word: *begun*. Now write its *last* letter. [Pause.] What letter did you write? Yes, *begun* ends with *n*. [Write *n* on the board.]

Now listen to the last letter of this word: *barber*. Write its *last* letter. [Pause.] What letter did you write? Yes, *r* is the last letter in *barber*. [Write the letter *r* on the board.]

[Proceed with the exercises that follow.]

1. Listen:

      down   beaten   explain

With what letter does each word end? Each one ends
with *n*. [Write *n*.] Listen carefully to some more words.
Write the *last letter* of each word that *does not* end with *n*.

addition	clean	tear	apron	ship
beaten	train	skin	down	star

What letters did you write? *R*, *p*, and *r* are right.
[Write these letters on the board.] *Tear* ends with *r*.
[Point.] *Ship* ends with *p*. [Point.] *Star* ends with *r*.

2. Listen:

stiff   beef   grief

With what letter does each word end? Each one ends
with *f*. [Write *f*.] Listen closely to the following words.
Write the *last letter* of each word that *does not* end with *f*.

leaf	thief	poor	off	proof
roof	answer	grain	deaf	loaf

What letters did you write? *R*, *r*, and *n* are right.
[Write the letters on the board.] *Answer* ends with *r*.
[Point.] *Poor* ends with *r*. *Grain* ends with *n*.

3. Listen:

minus   plus   hiss

With what letter does each end? Each one ends with
s. [Write *s*.] Listen closely to the following words. Write
the *last letter* of each word that *does not* end with *s*.

bus	circus	bother	chief
this	atlas	famous	address

What letters did you write? *R* and *f* are right. *Bother*
ends with *r* and *chief* ends with *f*. [Point.]

4. Listen:

> better   car   bar

With what letter does each end? Each one ends with *r*. [Write *r*.] Listen closely to the following words. Write the *last letter* of each word that *does not* end with *r*.

> anger   brother   another   butter   hoof
> star   water   glass   sister   danger

What letters did you write? *S* and *f* are right. [Write.] *Glass* ends with *s* and *hoof* ends with *f*. [Point.]

5. Listen:

> dim   drum   room

With what letter does each word end? Each one ends with *m*. [Write *m*.] Listen to the following words. Write the *last letter* of each word that *does not* end with *m*.

> ham   dream   ten   bedroom   hem
> puff   cram   ram   finger   jam

What letters did you write? *F*, *n*, and *r* are correct. [Write the letters.] *Puff* ends with *f*. [Point.] *Ten* ends with *n*. *Finger* ends with *r*.

6. Listen:

> bed   said   lead

With what letter does each word end? Each one ends with *d*. [Write *d*.] Listen to the following words. Write the *last letter* of each word that *does not* end with *d*.

> afraid   broad   team   head   bad
> raisin   bud   tread   dead   laid

What letters did you write? *N* and *m* are correct. [Write.] *Raisin* ends with *n* and *team* ends with *m*.

7. Listen:

> ball   boil   awful

With what letter does each word end? Each one ends with *l*. [Write *l*.] Listen to the following words. Write the *last letter* of each word that *does not* end with *l*.

> angel   careful   ram   animal   baseball
> haul   beautiful   lad   pail   cousin

What letters did you write? *M*, *d*, and *n* are right. [Write the letters.] *Ram* ends with *m*. *Lad* ends with *d*. *Cousin* ends with *n*.

8. Listen to these words:

> wait   cat   sit

With what letter does each word end? Yes, *t* is the last letter. [Write *t*.] Listen to the following words. Write the *last letter* of each word that *does not* end with *t*.

> shoot   banner   rabbit   bonnet   dream
> school   treat   violet   carried   boat

What letters did you write? *L*, *r*, *d*, and *m* are correct. *School* ends with *l*. *Banner* ends with *r*. *Carried* ends with *d*. *Dream* ends with *m*.

VISUAL IDENTIFICATION

[See that each child has Worksheet 4 before him. Call attention to rows 1–8, which accompany Lesson 5. Read the direction with the group. Then explain.]

I will write a word on the board. Look at it closely. When I erase it, find the same word in row 1 on your worksheet. Draw a circle around it.

[For each row, write the row number and the underlined word in that row. Count to five silently and erase the word.

1. afraid	apron	ahead	across
2. neat	lean	laid	leaf
3. unless	asleep	circus	address
4. baker	beak	paid	loaf
5. deer	dream	deep	forgot
6. ankle	am	avenue	braid
7. gases	bait	barrel	creep
8. cheap	pocket	scrub	twig

At the close of the lesson, direct a check of the children's responses. Again, write the correct word for each row on the board, with the number of the row before it. Have the children check their response in each row.]

Lesson 6

FINAL CONSONANTS:

p, b, g, k, x, z, c

[This lesson continues the work with final consonants. Direct the exercises as suggested in Lesson 5. Each child should have paper and pencil ready.]

AUDITORY IDENTIFICATION

Today you will learn more about letters and letter sounds at the ends of words.

1.   Listen to these words:

map   strip   stoop

With what letter does each one end? Yes, the letter is *p*. [Write *p* on the board.] Listen closely to each of the following words. Write the last letter of each word that *does not* end with *p*.

drop   heap   cloud   scrap   strap
carpet   leap   snap   group   chop

What letters did you write? *T* and *d* are right. [Write *t* and *d* on the board.] *Carpet* ends with *t*. [Point to *t*.] *Cloud* ends with *d*. [Point to *d*.]

2.   Listen to these words:

cab   rub   rob

With what letter does each word end? *B* is the last letter. [Write *b*.] Listen closely to each of the following words. Write the last letter of each word that *does not* end with *b*.

grab   stab   soap   club   grub
scrub   split   camel   crib   leaf

What letters did you write? *T*, *p*, *l*, and *f* are correct. [Write.] *Split* ends with *t*. [Point.] *Soap* ends with *p*. [Point.] *Camel* ends with the letter *l*. [Point.] *Lead* ends with *f*. [Point.]

Look at these words that end in *b:* [Write on board.]

climb bomb thumb lamb

comb limb crumb dumb

Who can pronounce these words? [Point to each word in turn and call on volunteers.] Now listen as I say each word. [Say each word.] Do you hear the *b* at the end? No. The *b* is *silent.* We call *b* in these words a *silent letter* because we do not sound the *b* or hear it.

3. Listen to these words:

beg twig drag

With what letter does each one end? *G* is the last letter. Listen closely to each of the following words. Write the last letter of each word that *does not* end with *g.*

rug jig drug club mug

bean flag swim frog wig

What letters did you write? *N, m,* and *b* are correct. *Bean* ends with *n. Swim* ends with *m. Club* ends with *b.*

4. Listen to these words:

leak soak cook

With what letter does each one end? *K* is the last letter. Listen closely to each of the following words. Write the last letter of each word that *does not* end with *k.*

hook creek job crook peak

steep speak brook hug steel

What letters did you write? *P, b, g,* and *l* are correct. [Write the letters.] *Steep* ends with *p.* [Point.] *Job* ends with *b. Hug* ends with *g. Steel* ends with *l.*

5. Listen to these words:

> ax   six   index

With what letter does each word end? X is the last letter. [Write x on the board.] Listen closely to each of the following words. Write the last letter of each word that *does not* end with x.

> box   ox   speak   wax
>
> mix   this   fix   fox

What letters did you write? S and k are correct. [Write s and k on the board.] *This* ends with s and *speak* ends with k.

6. Listen to these words:

> quiz   fez   topaz

With what letter does each one end? Z is the last letter. Listen closely to each of the following words. Write the last letter of each word that *does not* end with z.

> whiz   fuzz   jazz   buzz
>
> whiff   flax   jug   pass

What letters did you write? F, x, g, and s are correct. [Write.] *Whiff* ends with f. [Point.] *Flax* ends with x. *Jug* ends with g. *Pass* ends with s.

Sometimes a final s has a z sound. Listen to the s at the end of these words:

> his   apples   was   stairs   ashes

Can you think of other words that end with an s that sounds like z? [List words as children name them. They might name *has, does, goes, is, hers, days, tries, blows,* and others.]

7. Listen to these words:

comic   almanac   arithmetic

With what letter does each one end? *C* is the last letter. [Write *c*.]   Listen to the following words. Write the last letter of each word that *does not* end with *c*.

music   Pacific   ashes   public   index

picnic   pocket   attic   tonic   atomic

What letters did you write? *T*, *s*, and *x* are correct. *Pocket* ends with *t*. *Ashes* ends with *s*. *Index* ends with *x*.

VISUAL IDENTIFICATION

[This lesson is based on the second half of Worksheet 4. Call attention to rows 9 to 15. Read the direction with the group.]

I will write a row number and a word. Look at it closely. When I erase it, find the same word in row 9 on your worksheet. Draw a circle around it.

[For each row, write the row number and the underlined word in that row. Count five silently and then erase the word.

9.	creep	peak	cheer	steep	
10.	crib	good	grab	drag	
11.	float	flag	equal	crab	
12.	creek	shrub	seek	leak	
13.	instead	asleep	icebox	icicle	barrel
14.	quiz	crop	speak	whiz	strip
15.	coat	quiet	comic	streak	picnic

Direct a check of the children's responses. Write the correct number and word for each row on the board. Have the children check their responses.]

INITIAL BLENDS:

Lesson **7** | bl, cl, fl, gl, pl, sl;
sc, sm, sn, sp, st, sw

[Present the concept of the term **blend** as follows. On the board, write the three columns of words given below before beginning the exercises.]

Sometimes two letters go together to make the sound at the beginning of a word. Listen as I say the words in column 1.

1	2	3
black	clock	flag
blue	clear	flame
blank	climb	flash

Now say the words in column 1 after me. [Underline *bl* in each word as you say it.] What sound did you make and hear at the beginning of each word? Make that sound. [Point to *bl*.]

It takes two letters to make the sound *bl*. The sound that the two letters together make is called a **blend**.

Say the words in column 2 after me. [Underline *cl* in each word as you say it.] Give the sound of the blend *cl*.

[Repeat the procedure with column 3.]

AUDITORY DISCRIMINATION

1. Listen:

blade   bless   blind

With what blend do these three words begin? Yes, the blend *bl* is right. [Write *bl.*] Now I will say some more words. Some of them begin with *bl* and some begin with other blends. Listen for the words that *do not* begin with *bl.* Write the first two letters of those words.

blanket   clear   block   bless   blot
blew   bleed   bluff   flag   blink

What blends did you write? Yes, *cl* and *fl* are right. [Write *cl* and *fl* on the board.] *Clear* begins with *cl.* [Point to *cl.*] *Flag* begins with *fl.* [Point to *fl.*]

2. Listen:

cloud   close   clap

With what blend do these three words begin? Yes, with the blend *cl.* [Write the three words on the board and underline *cl.* Have the children say the words after you, sounding *cl* clearly.]

Listen again. I will say some more words. Some of them begin with the blend *cl* and some begin with other blends. Write the first two letters of the words that *do not* begin with *cl.*

class   clover   cloth   flash   click
closet   blade   clown   clay   clam

Which blends did you write? Yes, *bl* and *fl* are right. *Blade* begins with *bl.* *Flash* begins with *fl.* [Write the two words on the board. Underline the initial blends in each. Have the children say the words after you.]

3. Listen:

flat   flow   flour

With what blend do these words begin? Yes, *fl* is the blend. [Write *fl*.] Say each word after me.

Listen to these words. Write the first two letters of each word that *does not* begin with *fl*.

flit	float	flock	flood	flea
flesh	blown	closet	fleet	fly

What blends did you write? *Bl* and *cl* are right. [Write *blown* and *closet* and underline the blends.]

4. Listen to each of these words and think of the letters at the beginning:

glass   globe   glad

What two letters formed the blend at the beginning of each word? Yes, *gl*. [Write *gl* on the board. Have the children say the three words after you.] I am going to say some more words. Write the first two letters of each word that *does not* begin with the blend *gl*.

glide	glare	flower	glove	glow
clerk	blister	glisten	glue	gloomy

What blends did you write? *Cl*, *bl*, and *fl* are right. [Write *clerk*, *blister*, and *flower* and underline the blend in each.] *Clerk* begins with *cl*. [Point.] *Blister* begins with *bl*. *Flower* begins with *fl*.

5. Listen:

plain   plank   plate

With what blend do these words begin? Yes, *pl*. [Write the words and underline *pl*. Have the children

repeat the words after you.]   Listen to these words. Write
the beginning blend of each word that *does not* begin with
the letters *pl.*

| please | plan | fleet | plow | plane |
| plum | gloomy | plump | blow | play |

What blends did you write? Yes, *gl, fl,* and *bl* are right.
Gloomy begins with *gl. Fleet* begins with *fl. Blow* begins
with *bl.* [Write the three words on the board and underline the initial blend in each word. Have the children
repeat the three words.]

6. Listen:

slap   slave   sled

What blend did you hear at the beginning of each
word? Yes, *sl.* [Write the three words and underline *sl*
in each. Have the children repeat the words.]   Listen to
these words. Write the beginning blend of each word that
does not begin with *sl.*

| slice | sleep | please | slip | slope |
| slam | glue | sleeve | clip | sling |

What blends did you write? *Gl, pl,* and *cl* are right.
Glue begins with *gl. Please* begins with *pl. Clip* begins with
cl. [Write the three words and underline their blends.
Have the children repeat them after you.]

7. Listen to these words:

scatter   scale   scare

Say each word after me. With what blend does each
word begin? Each one begins with *sc.* [Write the words and

underline *sc.*]　Listen to the following words. Write the first two letters of each word that *does not* begin with *sc.*

<table>
<tr><td>scarce</td><td>scamp</td><td>place</td><td>scold</td><td>globe</td></tr>
<tr><td>slate</td><td>scarf</td><td>score</td><td>scooter</td><td>scout</td></tr>
</table>

What blends did you write? *Sl, pl,* and *gl* are right. *Slate* begins with *sl. Place* begins with *pl. Globe* begins with *gl.* [Write the three words, underline their initial blends, and have the children repeat the words after you.]

8.　Listen:

　　small　　smell　　smile

What two letters make the beginning sound in these words? Yes, the blend *sm* is right. Listen again. Write the beginning blend of each word that *does not* begin with the blend *sm.*

<table>
<tr><td>smart</td><td>smoke</td><td>smooth</td><td>slipper</td></tr>
<tr><td>smash</td><td>score</td><td>scout</td><td>smother</td></tr>
</table>

[Check pupils' responses as in preceding exercises.]

9.　Listen:

　　snow　　snap　　snore

What two letters make the beginning sound in these words? Yes, the blend *sn.* [Write the words, underline the initial blend in each, and have the children repeat the words after you.]　Listen again. Write the beginning blend of each word that *does not* begin with *sn.*

<table>
<tr><td>snail</td><td>snake</td><td>slip</td><td>sniff</td><td>snip</td></tr>
<tr><td>smell</td><td>speak</td><td>sneeze</td><td>scuff</td><td>snatch</td></tr>
</table>

[Check pupils' responses as in preceding exercises.]

10. Listen:

speak   space   spark

With what blend does each word begin? Yes, with *sp.* [Write the words and underline *sp*. Have the children repeat the words.]

Listen to the following words. Write the beginning blend of each word that *does not* begin with *sp*.

sparrow	spade	slim	spool	spot
spear	smear	speed	scoot	spout

[Check pupils' responses as in preceding exercises.]

11. Listen:

start   step   sting

[Ask the children to name the initial blend. Write the three words on the board and underline *st*. Have the children repeat the words after you as you underline the initial blend in each word.]

Listen to the following words. Write the beginning blend of each word that *does not* begin with the blend *st*.

stoop	starch	spill	station	stage
steep	sniff	starve	small	scale

[Check pupils' responses as in preceding exercises.]

12. Listen:

swim   swift   switch

[Ask the children to name the initial blend. Then write the three words on the board and underline *sw* in each word. Have the children repeat the words after you.]

Listen again. Write the beginning blend of each word that *does not* begin with *sw*.

swamp	swell	slept	smart	steep
swim	spell	swept	swoop	sweep

[Check pupil's responses as in preceding exercises.]

VISUAL DISCRIMINATION

[Have the children turn to Worksheet 5 and read the directions as you read aloud.]

Look at the two columns of words in box 1. Point to the first word in the left column. [See that all children are pointing correctly. Ask them to name the word *blade*.] Underline the first two letters in *blade*. Point to a word in the right column of box 1 that begins with the same letters. [See that all children are pointing to *blue*. Have them name the word.] Draw a line from *blade* to *blue* to show that they begin with the same blend, *bl.* [If necessary, repeat for *clown* and *close*.]

In box 1, draw a line from each word in the left column to a word in the right column that begins with the same blend. Then do the same thing in box 2.

[Here are the correct responses:]

1.

2.

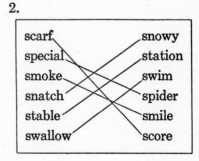

[Direct a check of the worksheets. Call on a child to name the word that begins like *blade, clown,* and so on. The checks may be given after the completion of each box or of both boxes, depending on how much guidance the children need.]

Lesson **8**	**INITIAL BLENDS:** br, cr, dr, fr, gr, pr, tr; ch, sh, th, wh; spr, str, thr

AUDITORY DISCRIMINATION: TWO-LETTER BLENDS

[See that children have paper and pencils ready.]

In this lesson you will learn about more words that begin with blends.

1. Listen to these words:

> bridge   brave   brass

What two letters did you hear at the beginning of each word? Yes, the letters *br*. [Write the words and underline *br*.] Listen again. Write the beginning letters of any words that *do not* begin with the blend *br*.

> branch   brand   break   brought   blade
> breast   glad   swing   score   broad

What blends did you write? Yes, the blends *gl*, *sw*, *sc*, and *bl* are right. [Write these words on the board.] *Glad* begins with *gl*. [Point.] *Swing* begins with *sw*. *Score* begins with *sc*. *Blade* begins with *bl*. [Have the children repeat these words after you.]

2. Listen:

      crack   crash   creek

[As before, ask the children to identify the initial letters *cr*. Write the three words and underline initial blend *cr*.]

Listen to the following words. Think which words *do not* begin with the blend *cr* like *crack* and *crash*. Write the beginning blend of each word that *does not* begin with *cr*.

cradle	creep	brook	crow	crop
crawl	clock	crook	snap	crowd

[Proceed as in exercise 1 to help the children check their written responses. They should have written *cl* (for *clock*), *br* (for *brook*), and *sn* (for *snap*).]

3. Listen:

      drag   draw   drown

What two letters did you hear at the beginning of each word? Yes, all of these words begin with the blend *dr*. [Write the three words and underline initial blend *dr*. Have the children repeat the words after you.]

[Direct the children to listen as you dictate the following words and to write the two letters that begin each word that *does not* begin with *dr*.]

drop	dream	drove	bless	flow
draw	cream	broke	dresser	drug

[Proceed as directed in previous exercises to help children check their written responses. Write *cream*, *broke*, *bless*, and *flow* on the board, underline the initial blends, and have the children say each word after you.]

4. Listen:

   froze   Friday   frog

[Ask children to identify the initial blend of these three words. Write the words and underline initial *fr* in each. Have children repeat the words.]

Listen to these words. Write the initial blend of each word that *does not* begin with *fr*.

frame	free	dried	freeze	crown
friend	steep	fried	breeze	front

What blends did you write? [As children name them, write the words *steep*, *dried*, *breeze*, and *crown* on the board and underline the initial blend of each. Have the children say each word after you.]

5. Listen:

   grand   gravy   grape

[Question children to help them identify the letters in the initial blend *gr*. Write the words and underline *gr*. Repeat each word to develop recognition of the *gr* sound.

Dictate the following words, asking children to write the initial blend of each word that *does not* begin with *gr*.]

grade	grease	break	grocery	group
crumb	fraction	greet	driver	growl

What blends did you write? *Cr*, *fr*, *br*, and *dr* are right. [Write *crumb*, *fraction*, *break*, and *driver* and underline the

initial blend in each. Have children say each word as you
underline the blend.]

6. Listen:

> pray   price   prove

With what two letters does each word begin? Each
one begins with the blend *pr*. [Write the three words on
the board and underline the initial blend in each. Have the
children say the words.]

Listen to each word I say. Write the first two letters
in each word that *does not* begin with *pr*.

> practice   proud   prize   praise   promise
> press   ground   drive   bruise   print

What letters did you write? *Gr*, *dr*, and *br* are correct.
Ground begins with *gr*. *Drive* begins with *dr*. *Bruise* begins
with *br*. [Write the three words on the board and point to
the initial blend in each. If more practice seems desirable,
say each of the eight words again, have the children repeat
them after you, and point out the difference in sounds of
the initial blends.]

7. Listen:

> trap   tramp   travel

With what two letters do these words begin? Each one
begins with *tr*. [Write the words, underline the initial
blend, and have children repeat the words. Pronounce the
following words and instruct the children to write the first
two letters of each word that *does not* begin with *tr*.]

> trailer   trace   trap   trouble   truth
> trapper   grade   track   protect   fruit

[Have the children name the blends they wrote. Then write *grade, protect,* and *fruit* on the board. Underline the initial blend. Contrast with *tr* in the other words. Have the children repeat the *tr* words after you.]

[Note: If it seems advisable, defer exercises 8–14 until another period. If they are deferred, review the idea of the initial blend as suggested at the beginning of Lesson 7 on page 29 before taking up exercise 8.]

8.   Listen:

chase   chain   chart

With what two letters does each word begin? Each word begins with the blend *ch.*   [Write *ch* on the board.]
Listen to the following words. Write the first two letters of each word that *does not* begin with *ch.*

chosen	creek	chop	chalk	treat
frozen	cheek	drop	chick	church

What blends did you write? *Fr, cr, dr,* and *tr* are right. [Write *frozen, creek, drop,* and *treat* and underline the initial blends. Have the children repeat the *ch* words after you.]

9. [Present initial blend *sh,* following the procedure in the preceding exercises. Use the following words for presenting and identifying initial *sh.*

sharp   shake   sheet

Use the following list of words for identification of blends other than *sh.*

shade	shirt	shadow	shout	price
shine	china	shoot	cross	share]

[Check on accuracy of children's identification of initial blends differing from *sh*, as suggested in previous exercises. They should have written *ch*, *cr*, and *pr*. Have the children repeat the seven *sh* words after you.]

10. Listen:

> thick   thousand   thirsty

[Ask the children to name the letters that form the initial blend. Have them say the words after you. Write the words and underline *th* in each.]

Listen as I say some more words. Write the first two letters of each word that *does not* begin with the blend *th*.

> thunder   third   thankful   thin   thumb
>
> Thursday   shirt   cheerful   theater   truck

[Discuss children's responses as suggested in previous exercises. They should have written *sh* (*shirt*), *ch* (*cheerful*), and *tr* (*truck*). Have the group repeat the *th* words after you.]

[Explain that *th* has another sound.] When you say *thin*, you do not hear your voice when you sound the blend *th*. Say *thin*. [Pause.] Now say *then*. Do you hear your voice when you say the *th* in *then*? Say the words in each pair after me. Notice the difference between the *th* sounds in each pair. [Say each pair aloud, emphasizing the initial sounds. Have the children repeat after you.]

> thank — than   thought — though
>
> thin — this   thirsty — those
>
> third — these   thunder — themselves
>
> thumb — them   thing — their

11. Listen:

> whip   whale   why

With what two letters do these words begin? Yes, with *wh*. [Write the words and underline *wh*.] Say each word after me. Listen for the blend *wh*.

Listen to these words. Write the first two letters of each word that *does not* begin with *wh*.

> whisper   whenever   wheel   where   wheat
> whistle   thirteen   sheet   there   white

[Check as in previous exercises. The children should have written *th* (*thirteen*), *sh* (*sheet*), and *th* (*there*).]

THREE-LETTER BLENDS

12. Some words begin with three letters that go together to make a single sound. That is, there are three-letter blends at the beginning of some words. Listen to the following words:

> sprain   spruce   spring

Say each word after me. [Repeat words.] What three letters did you hear at the beginning of each word? Yes, this three-letter blend is *spr*. [Write the words and underline *spr* in each word.] Listen to these words. Write the first three letters of any word that *does not* begin with *spr*.

> spread   strung   sprinkle   thrush
> sprang   sprung   spray   sprawl

What letters did you write? *Str* and *thr* are right. Write *strung* and *thrush* and underline the initial blend in each word.

13. Listen:

strange   straight   stretch

[Have children say each word after you.] What three letters make the sound at the beginning of each word? Yes, *str*. [Write the words and underline *str*.]

Listen to these words. Write the first three letters of any word that *does not* begin with *str*.

street	stray	strip	thread	strut
string	spray	stripe	struck	streak

What letters did you write? *Spr* and *thr* are correct. *Spray* begins with *spr*. [Write *spray* and underline *spr*.] *Thread* begins with *thr*. [Write *thread* and underline *thr*. Have the group pronounce the *str* words after you.]

14. Listen:

thrill   thrash   throat

[As before, have children repeat the words after you and name the initial three letters. Then write the words and underline *thr* in each.]

Listen to these words. Write the first three letters of each word that *does not* begin with *thr*.

throw	thrift	threw	spread	thresh
three	stream	through	thread	throb

What letters did you write? *Str* and *spr* are right. *Stream* begins with *str*. [Write *stream* and underline *str*.] *Spread* begins with *spr*. [Write *spread* and underline *spr*. Have the children repeat the *thr* words after you.]

VISUAL IDENTIFICATION

[Have the children turn to Worksheet 6. Read the direction with the group.]

Look at row 1 on your worksheet. I will write one of the words in row 1 on the board. Look at it closely, for I shall erase it. Find that word in row 1 and draw a circle around it. I will do the same for each row. Look up when you have found and circled the word.

[Write each row number before the underlined word in that row. Count five before you erase the word. Before you write, be sure to have the full attention of the class.

1. <u>chain</u>	class	shine	thank	white
2. skate	swim	<u>shout</u>	spell	sail
3. chick	<u>thirty</u>	tribe	wheel	sling
4. flame	blame	dream	<u>frame</u>	train
5. dress	blaze	<u>brass</u>	grass	drank
6. crop	drop	trail	thin	<u>trap</u>
7. <u>wheat</u>	tribe	thick	chest	these
8. friend	breast	<u>dream</u>	crown	print
9. trade	<u>grape</u>	tramp	frank	prank
10. trim	grind	crime	<u>prince</u>	bring
11. freeze	<u>cream</u>	prize	gravy	shadow
12. spray	sting	strap	trash	<u>threw</u>
13. <u>spring</u>	brain	chalk	whisper	thread
14. straw	spread	<u>strange</u>	throat	share

Have each child check his own responses. On the board, write each row number with the correct word for each row; that is, the underlined word above.]

FINAL BLENDS:

Lesson 9 | st, nt, rt, lt, ft, ct, pt;
nd, rd, ld; rl, rn, rm, mp

AUDITORY IDENTIFICATION

[With this lesson, there is a shift from initial to final blends. Each child should have paper and pencil ready. Then present the following explanation.]

You have learned that sometimes two or three letters together make a single sound. Such letters form a *blend*. In the last two lessons you listened for and wrote blends that come at the beginnings of words. Now you will listen for and write some blends that come at the *ends* of words.

I am going to say a word, and you are to say it after me. See whether you can tell me the last two letters in the word. [Say each word distinctly.]

Listen: *best*. Now say the word after me and think about the last two letters: *best*. [Pause.] What two letters did you hear at the end of *best?* Yes, the blend *st*. [Write *best* on the board and underline *st*.]

Listen: *sent*. Say *sent*. [Pause.] What two letters did you hear at the end? Yes, the blend *nt*. [Write *sent* and underline *nt*.] Does everyone understand? Then you are ready for the exercises.

1. Listen:

> west   coast   chest

With what two letters does each word end? Right, *st*. [Write the words and underline *st*.] I will say some other words. Listen closely to each word. Write the last two letters of any word that does not end with the letters *st*.

toast	rent	dust	best	list
post	mist	roast	hunt	rust

Which letters did you write? *Nt* is correct. *Rent* and *hunt* end with *nt*. [Write the words and underline *nt*. Have the children say the words.]

2. Listen to the following words. Write the last two letters of each word that does not end in *nt*.

front	silent	absent	contest	bent
stunt	waist	against	point	pint

What did you write? *St* is correct. *Waist, against*, and *contest* end with *st*. [Write the words and underline the final blend *st*. Have the children repeat the words.]

3. Listen to the following words:

> cart   heart   hurt

With what two letters does each word end? Each ends with the blend *rt*. [Write *rt*.] Listen to the following words. Write the last two letters in each word that does not end with the letters *rt*.

part	seaport	quart	report	trust
shirt	tent	art	skirt	sport

What did you write? The blends *nt* and *st* are right. *Tent* [Write on the board.] ends with *nt*. [Underline *nt*.] *Trust* [Write.] ends with *st*. [Underline *st*.]

4. Say the following words after me:

      belt   felt   quilt

With what two letters does each word end? Each one ends with the blend *lt*. [Write *lt* on the board.] Write the last two letters in each of the following words that does not end with the blend *lt*.

melt	sent	quart	fault	bolt
salt	built	colt	instant	guilt

What letters did you write? *Nt* and *rt* are correct. *Sent* and *instant* end with *nt*. *Quart* ends with *rt*. [Write the three words and underline their final blends.]

5. Say the following words after me:

      lift   soft   swift

With what two letters does each one end? Each word ends with the letters *ft*. [Write *ft* on the board.] Listen to the following words. Write the last two letters in each word that does not end with *ft*.

left	forest	raft	halt	waft
sift	drift	paint	thrift	draft

What did you write? *St*, *nt*, and *lt* are right. *Forest* ends with *st*. *Paint* ends with *nt*. *Halt* ends with *lt*. [Write the three words and underline their final blends.]

6. Say the following words after me:

      act   respect   direct

With what two letters does each one end? Each one ends with the blend *ct*. [Write *ct* on the board.] Write the last two letters in each of the following words that does not end with *ct*.

protect	result	conduct	exact	contact
connect	fact	report	draft	detect

What did you write? *Lt*, *rt*, and *ft* are correct. *Result* ends with *lt*. *Report* ends with *rt*. *Draft* ends with *ft*. [Write the three words and underline their final blends.]

7. Say the following words after me:

kept   accept   except

With what two letters does each one end? Each one ends with the letters *pt*. [Write *pt* on the board.] Write the last two letters in each of the following words that does not end with *pt*.

slept	apt	select	shaft
swept	fact	crept	heart

What did you write? *Ct*, *ft*, and *rt* are right. [Write *fact*, *select*, *shaft*, and *heart* and underline the final blends.]

[Note: If it seems desirable, present the remaining exercises at a later period.]

8. Listen to the following words:

friend   bend   errand

With what two letters does each end? Each word ends with *nd*. [Write *nd* on the board.] Write the last two letters in each of the following words that does not end with the blend *nd*.

grand	wept	brand	mind
pound	collect	lend	pond

What did you write? *Pt* and *ct* are correct. [Write *wept* and *collect* and underline the final blend in each. Have children repeat the words.]

9. Say the following words after me:

    cord   heard   third

With what two letters does each end? Each ends with the blend *rd*. [Write *rd* on the board.] Write the last two letters in each of the following words that does not end with the blend *rd*.

word	sword	reward	spent	yard
find	card	record	loft	board

What did you write? *Nd, nt,* and *ft* are correct. [Write *find, spent,* and *loft* and underline the final blends. Have children repeat the words.]

10. Say the following words after me:

    bold   child   cold

With what two letters does each word end? Yes, each word ends with *ld*. [Write *ld* on the board.] Write the last two letters in each of the following words that does not end with the blend *ld*.

mold	told	fold	held	heard
grind	old	wild	mild	kept

What did you write? *Nd, rd,* and *pt* are correct. *Grind* ends with *nd*. *Heard* ends with *rd*. *Kept* ends with *pt*. [Write the three words and underline their final blends.]

11. Say the following words after me:

hurl   curl   pearl

With what two letters does each word end? Yes, with *rl*. [Write *rl* on the board.]   Write the last two letters in each of the following words that does not end with *rl*.

earl   whirl   hold   girl   melt

What did you write? *Ld* and *lt* are correct.   [Write *hold* and *melt* and underline their final blends.]

12. Say the following words after me:

born   yarn   horn

With what two letters does each end? Each ends with the blend *rn*.   [Write *rn*.]   Write the last two letters in each of the following words that does not end with *rn*.

earn   popcorn   twirl   return   worn
burn   scold   attend   learn   pattern

What did you write? *Ld, rl,* and *nd* are correct.   [Write *scold, twirl,* and *attend* and underline their final blends.]

13. Say the following words after me:

arm   warm   storm

With what two letters does each one end? Each one ends with the final blend *rm*.   [Write *rm* on the board.] Write the last two letters of each of the following words that does not end with *rm*.

worm   farm   firm   term
form   stern   orchard   germ

What blends did you write? *Rn* and *rd* are correct.

[Write *stern* and *orchard* and underline their final blends. Have children repeat the words.]

14. Listen:

jump   bump   romp

Say the words after me and listen for the last two letters. What letters did you hear? Yes, *mp.* [Write the words and underline *mp.*] Listen to these words. Write the last two letters of each word that does not end in *mp.*

pump   whirl   limp   harm

stamp   lump   wept   lamp

What letters did you write? *Rl, pt,* and *rm* are correct. [Write *whirl, wept,* and *harm* and underline the final blends. Have children repeat the words.]

VISUAL AND AUDITORY MEMORY

[The work that follows requires the exercise of (*a*) visual memory of a written word, and (*b*) auditory memory of the final blends presented in the lesson. Use your discretion as to the number of lists (word groups) you will use in a single period. It is suggested that set I be used in one period, set II in a second period, and set III in a third period.

Each child should have paper and pencil ready. See page 52. Have children write the list numbers 1, 2, 3, 4, 5 on their papers, showing them how to place the numbers. Have those numbers on the board also.]

Today you will write five lists of words that end with the blends that you have just listened to and written.

I am going to write the first word in list 1 on the board. Watch closely as I write it, for I will erase it in five seconds. Then you are to write the word on your paper. [Write *past* under 1, count silently to five, and then erase the word.] Now write the word that I wrote.

There will be a number of words. Have sharp eyes. In every five words, four end with the same blend. There will be one that ends with a different blend. Be sure to notice that one.

[After each group of five words has been written, stop for a check. Pronounce and spell each word, and have the children check the words they have written. Note the children that make mistakes, and help clear up the difficulty that caused the error.

I

1	2	3	4	5
past	lift	built	tent	board
list	raft	melt	bent	send
test	drift	west	soft	third
hurt	post	felt	silent	reward
mist	thrift	quilt	front	orchard

II

1	2	3	4	5
point	whirl	farm	bend	part
conduct	girl	court	friend	pound
object	curl	worm	card	skirt
select	pearl	storm	lend	heart
fact	colt	harm	mind	smart

III

1	2	3	4	5
learn	kept	errand	wild	bump
return	slept	frost	fold	storm
hurt	court	second	mild	camp
burn	except	tend	mend	lamp
worn	wept	send	bold	pump]

FINAL BLENDS:

Lesson 10 | lf, lp, th, sh, ch;
rth, tch, rch, nch

AUDITORY IDENTIFICATION

[Each child should have paper and pencil ready.]

Now you will work with more words that end with blends. Be ready for the first exercise.

1. I am going to say three words. I will pause after each one so that you can say it after me.

> gulf   self   wolf

With what two letters does each word end? Each word ends with *lf*. [Write the words and underline *lf* in each.]

Write the last two letters in each of the following words that does not end with the blend *lf*.

> herself   shelf   melt   myself
>
> swift   itself   elf   belt

What did you write? *Ft* and *lt* are correct. *Swift* ends with *ft*. *Melt* and *belt* end with *lt*. [Write the two words and underline the final blends. Have the children repeat the words after you.]

2. Listen to the following words:

> help   scalp   pulp

With what two letters does each word end? Each word ends with *lp*. [Write *lp* on the board and have the group repeat the three words after you.]

Write the last two letters in each of the following words that does not end with the blend *lp*:

> yelp   pulp   slept   help

What did you write? *Pt* is correct. *Slept* ends with *pt*. [Write the word, underline *pt*, and have the children say the word.]

3. You have worked with the blend *th* at the beginning of a word. Sometimes *th* is at the end of a word. Listen:

> both   cloth   beneath

With what two letters does each word end? Right, *th*. [Write *th* on the board.] Write the last two letters in each of the following words that does not end with *th*.

> wreath   south   breath   truth   fish
>
> bath   teeth   mouth   shelf   path

What did you write? *Lf* and *sh* are correct. *Shelf* ends with *lf*. *Fish* ends with *sh*. [Write the words and underline the final blends. Have children say them.]

4. Listen to the following words:

> fish   bush   flash

With what two letters does each end? Each ends with *sh*. [Write *sh* on the board.] Listen again. Write the last two letters in each of the following words that does not end with *sh*.

cash	moth	brush	push	polish
dish	crush	gulf	wish	help

What did you write? *Th, lf,* and *lp* are correct. *Moth* ends with *th. Gulf* ends with *lf. Help* ends with *lp.* [Write the three words and underline the final blends.]

5. Listen:

rich   teach   beach

With what two letters does each word end? Yes, each word ends with the blend *ch.* [Write *ch.*] Listen to the following words. Write the last two letters in each word that does not end with *ch.*

touch	splash	such	which
reach	each	both	gulf

What did you write? *Sh, th,* and *lf* are right. *Splash* ends with *sh. Both* ends with *th. Gulf* ends with *lf.* [Write the three words and underline their final blends.]

6. Some words end with the sound (or blend) of three letters. Listen to the last three letters of these words:

earth   north   fourth

What letters did you hear? *Rth* is correct. [Write the three words and underline *rth.* Do not erase them.]

7. Here are other words that end with the sound of three letters. Listen and tell me the last three letters of these words:

catch   Dutch   stitch   switch

What are the last three letters of each? *Tch* is correct.

[Write the words and underline final *tch* in each. Have the children compare the *rth* and *tch* endings. Then have them repeat the *rth* and *tch* words after you.]

Listen to the following words. Write the last three letters in each word that does not end with *tch*.

pitch	scratch	hatch	catch	ditch
worth	birth	match	fourth	witch

What did you write? *Rth* is correct. *Worth*, *birth*, and *fourth* end with *rth*. [Write these words and underline *rth* in each. Have children repeat the words.]

8. Listen:

   march   church   birch

With what three letters does each word end? Right, each word ends with *rch*. [Write the words and underline the blend *rch* in each. Have the group repeat the words.]

Listen to the following words. Write the last three letters in each word that does not end with *rch*.

scorch	torch	church	match
starch	north	earth	march

What did you write? *Rth* and *tch* are correct. *North* and *earth* end with *rth*. *Match* ends with *tch*. [Write the words and underline their final blends. Have children repeat the words.]

9. Listen:

   inch   bench   bunch

With what three letters does each word end? Right, each ends with *nch*. [Write the words and underline *nch*.]

Listen to the following words. Write the last three letters of each word that does not end with *nch*.

    lunch   ditch   finch   crunch   switch

What did you write? *Tch* is correct. *Ditch* and *switch* end with *tch*. [Write the words and underline *tch*.]

10. On your paper, write the last *three* letters of each of the following words. [Dictate number and word.]

1. patch   3. fourth   5. bench   7. church
2. march   4. inch   6. earth   8. catch

[At the close, write each word on the board, underline the final blends, and direct the children to check their own list of blends.]

11. Write the last *two* letters of each of the following words after I say it. [Dictate number and word.]

1. such   3. much   5. goldfish
2. south   4. beneath 6. dish

[At the close, write each word, underline its final blend, and direct the children to check their responses.]

VISUAL AND AUDITORY IDENTIFICATION

[Each child should have paper and pencil ready. Note the lists of words on page 58, and show children how to number and arrange the lists of words you are going to dictate.]

Today you will work with more words in which the last letters form a blend that makes a single sound. Some words will have two-letter blends at the end and some will have three-letter blends at the end. Watch closely as I write a word. I will erase it in five seconds. Then you are to write the word on your paper.

There will be four words in each list. Three of them end with the same blend. The other one ends with a different blend. After you have written the four words, I will say each word and spell it. Check your words to see that they are spelled correctly.

[Dictate both number and word, and have children write the number as well as the word. After each list of words, stop for a check. Pronounce and spell each word and have the children check each word they have written. Note the children who make mistakes, and help them to clear up their difficulty.

If desirable, use set I at one period and set II at another period.

I

1	2	3	4	5
1. shelf	1. scalp	1. reach	1. bush	1. mouth
2. gulf	2. gulp	2. such	2. both	2. teeth
3. help	3. yelp	3. truth	3. brush	3. teach
4. elf	4. wolf	4. touch	4. crush	4. cloth

II

1	2	3	4
1. bench	1. north	1. watch	1. starch
2. lunch	2. earth	2. branch	2. finch
3. inch	3. catch	3. patch	3. church
4. birch	4. fourth	4. ditch	4. search]

Lesson 11 | ## VOWELS AND VOWEL SOUNDS

AUDITORY IDENTIFICATION: SHORT AND LONG VOWELS

[The diacritical marks used in this lesson are those used in Webster's *New International Dictionary*, Second Edition, Unabridged.

Before taking up this lesson, prepare a table or key of the short and long vowel sounds like the one below.

Short Sounds	Long Sounds
ă as in măt ————————→	ā as in māte
ĕ as in wĕt ————————→	ē as in wē
ĭ as in bĭt ————————→	ī as in bīte
ŏ as in nŏt ————————→	ō as in nōte
ŭ as in ŭs ————————→	ū as in ūse

Place the key either on a manila chart sheet or on a part of the board where it may be preserved for use in connection with various exercises involving vowel sounds. Introduce the lesson on vowels as follows.]

You have been working with letters that you hear and see at the beginnings and endings of some words. The letters you have been working with are *consonants*. Today's lesson will be about five letters of another kind. They are the *vowels* in the alphabet. Here are the five vowels. [Write them on the board, and name each vowel as you write it.]

a   e   i   o   u

Each of these vowels has several different sounds. Here is a key [Point to the board or display the chart.] that tells about the *short sound* and the *long sound* of each vowel. Listen closely and repeat what I say. I will say the short sound and the long sound of each vowel.

[Place a ruler or cardboard across the bottom of each line and read across the line, as: "ă as in măt — ā as in māte." Emphasize the change in position of the lips and teeth as you repeat each word to bring out the difference between the two vowel sounds. Have the children do the same.]

Did you notice that the long sound of a vowel is the same as the name of the vowel? Say the short and long sound of each vowel after me, and you will hear why the two sounds are called *short* and *long*. [Write the following on the board. Then say each sound, pointing to the letter as you say its sound.]

ă-ā   ĕ-ē   ĭ-ī   ŏ-ō   ŭ-ū

The letter *y* can be used as a vowel. It may have the sound of long *i*, as in these words:

bȳ (*bī*)   mȳ (*mī*)   trȳ (*trī*)   stȳle (*stīle*)

It may have the sound of short *i*, as in these words:

mȳth (*mĭth*) ladȳ (*ladĭ*) sȳcamore (*sĭc*) sȳllable (*sĭl*)

[Direct the following exercises.]

1. I am going to say some pairs of names. Each name begins with a vowel. I will ask different boys and girls to say each pair of names after me and tell whether the beginning vowel in each name has the short sound or the long sound. Look at the key if you need help.

[Call on individual children.

Amy	— Alice	Asia	— Alps
Ethel	— Edith	Everest	— Egypt
Isabel	— Irene	India	— Iceland
Ona	— Oscar	Oregon	— Ohio
Undine	— Ulysses	Utah	— Ulster]

2. [Have the children take out a sheet of paper and a pencil. Direct them to write the numbers from 1 to 30 on their papers. Then proceed as follows.]

Each word that I am going to say begins with a vowel. The vowel may have either the short or long sound.

I will say a number and a word, like this: "Number 1 — ice." Listen to the sound of the beginning vowel. Say the word after me and think which vowel begins *ice*. [Pause.] Now write that vowel after the number 1 on your paper. [Pause.] Which vowel did you write? Yes, the vowel *i* is correct.

Listen again: "2 — odd." Say the word *odd*. [Pause.] Now write its beginning vowel after *2* on your paper.

[Continue with the rest of the words in the same manner.

1. ice	6. able	11. edge	16. even	21. until	26. apple
2. odd	7. emu	12. act	17. ivy	22. if	27. uncle
3. egg	8. ankle	13. ink	18. obey	23. ill	28. empty
4. age	9. open	14. object	19. ate	24. idea	29. equal
5. use	10. useful	15. upset	20. usual	25. olive	30. old

Direct a check after each five words. Give the number, the word, and the name of the beginning vowel. Have the children check to see whether they wrote the correct vowel.]

3. [To provide more practice on the vowel sounds, use the words in exercise 2 again. Say a word. Call on a child to name the beginning vowel and tell whether the vowel has the short or long sound. Refer to the key of sounds when help is needed.]

4. [Ask the children to take out paper and pencil.] Listen to this word: *lamp.* Can you hear the vowel in the middle of *lamp?* What is that vowel? Yes, the vowel is *a.* Is it short *a* or long *a?* Yes, it is short *a.*

I will name some other words. Listen for the vowel in the middle of each word. Then write that vowel after the right number on your paper. [Dictate the following:

1. bus	6. cute	11. frog	16. dude
2. fish	7. hold	12. bat	17. Pete
3. top	8. late	13. sit	18. hole
4. hand	9. pile	14. bed	19. rice
5. cup	10. pave·	15. leg	20. key

After each five words, direct a check. Write each word, with its number, on the board. Ask the children to name the vowel in the middle of the word, and then check to see whether they wrote the right vowel on their papers.]

5. [Have the children turn to Worksheet 7. Read the directions with the group. Be sure that they understand the vowel markings. Demonstrate with the first two or three words what is to be done. Check after each five words. Write each word, its number, and the correct vowel mark on the board. Have the children check their own words.

Here are the words with the correct vowel marks:

1. hăd	6. mĭlk	11. blŏck	16. jŭmp	21. bē
2. pĭg	7. bănd	12. ĕnd	17. stŏp	22. līne
3. bīte	8. hĕlp	13. fŭn	18. fāce	23. tūbe
4. āpe	9. clāy	14. bŭnch	19. rīce	24. shē
5. gĕt	10. pōle	15. hōpe	20. tūne	25. rănch]

Lesson 12 | COMPOUND WORDS

Some words, such as *lighthouse*, are made up of two words. Such a word is called a **compound word**. In a short paragraph that I am going to read to you, you will hear six compound words. Listen closely. Be ready to tell me some compound words that you heard. [Read.]

This afternoon we boys played baseball on the playground. I was first baseman and my brother Tom was shortstop. In my first turn at bat, I made a fine hit but the ball was caught by a boy in the outfield.

[As the children name them, write the compound words on the board as shown below.

afternoon = after + noon
baseball = base + ball
playground = play + ground
baseman = base + man
shortstop = short + stop
outfield = out + field]

WRITING FROM VISUAL MEMORY

[See that the children have paper and pencils ready.]

I am going to write two words on the board. [Write *news* and *paper*.] Say the two words to yourself as one

long word, or compound word. [Pause.] Now I will
erase the words. [Erase.] Write the two words together
to make a compound word. [After children have had time
to write, write the word *newspaper* on the board and ask
them to check the word they wrote.]

Do you understand? If you do, you are ready to begin
the exercise.

[Write the two words that form each of the 24 compound
words listed below. After each list of 8 words, check with the
children by writing each compound word and its number on the
board and directing them to check the word that they have
written.]

1. bookmark	9. horseback	17. songbird
2. cardboard	10. highway	18. chairman
3. icebox	11. tiptoe	19. firecracker
4. workman	12. hardwood	20. goldfish
5. bedroom	13. birthday	21. policeman
6. anybody	14. washroom	22. overcoat
7. bookcase	15. milkman	23. notebook
8. daylight	16. sidewalk	24. everyone
(Check)	(Check)	(Check)

AUDITORY IDENTIFICATION

[Have the children turn to Worksheet 8. Read the direction
for the exercise for Lesson 12 with the group.]

This exercise will show you whether you have sharp
ears and sharp eyes. First, look at your worksheet. Do you
see the three words after each number? I am going to say
a compound word that has one of the words in row 1 in it.
I will say: "1. fireplace." Find part of that word in row 1.
Draw a circle around it. [Check the responses.]

[Proceed in the same way through row 24. The rows on the worksheet and the compound word are given below. Check after rows 8, 16, and 24 by repeating the compound word for the row and then writing on the board the word to be circled, underlined below. Have the children check their own responses.

Dictated Word

1. fish	maple	fire	1. fireplace
2. bank	ball	bake	2. football
3. list	leaf	less	3. careless
4. light	cash	linen	4. flashlight
5. act	place	plane	5. airplane
6. week	weeds	wheel	6. weekday
7. tire	been	time	7. bedtime
8. kind	hole	hold	8. keyhole
9. hook	hero	home	9. homework
10. board	beast	bound	10. billboard
11. able	ache	class	11. headache
12. over	shot	once	12. overshoe
13. shall	milk	shelf	13. bookshelf
14. door	poor	does	14. doorway
15. black	note	not	15. notebook
16. gulf	flash	fish	16. goldfish
17. pole	port	paste	17. airport
18. fly	floor	try	18. firefly
19. gum	gone	gun	19. gunboat
20. yard	word	bird	20. blackbird
21. deer	down	harm	21. downstairs
22. grew	gown	green	22. evergreen
23. while	where	whip	23. somewhere
24. snow	slow	soak	24. snowflake]

Lesson *13* | COMPOUND WORDS

WRITING FROM VISUAL MEMORY

[See that children have paper and pencils ready. Write on the board the two words that form each compound word below; as, 1. tea – – – cup. Direct the children to say the two words together silently. Then have them write the number and the compound word.

1. teacup	9. sunshine	17. footstool
2. beehive	10. moonbeam	18. snakeweed
3. haircut	11. woodland	19. horseback
4. footstep	12. drumstick	20. strawberry
5. windmill	13. bluebird	21. gingerbread
6. anybody	14. daylight	22. popcorn
7. overnight	15. cupcake	23. railroad
8. basketball	16. schoolhouse	24. pancake

Check after each eight words as suggested for Lesson 12.]

AUDITORY IDENTIFICATION

[Have the children turn to Worksheet 8.]

Today you will be word detectives again, just as you were when you worked on the front of Worksheet 8. Turn the worksheet over and find the exercise for Lesson 13.

[Proceed as directed in Lesson 12. Give the row number and say the compound word twice. Direct the children to circle, in the row named, the word that they heard in the compound word. The words to be dictated and the words on the worksheet, follow. After each 8 words, check as directed in Lesson 12.

Dictated Word

1. nail	mail	rail	1. railroad
2. pile	pole	pane	2. flagpole
3. bank	band	board	3. billboard
4. hand	hair	head	4. hairbrush
5. mouth	move	mouse	5. mousetrap
6. way	wag	bay	6. driveway
7. people	pile	pick	7. woodpile
8. hook	cost	cook	8. cookbook
9. limb	lone	line	9. headline
10. store	skate	story	10. drugstore
11. bold	boy	toy	11. cowboy
12. town	down	done	12. downfall
13. wash	wish	fish	13. fishhook
14. wall	walk	work	14. sidewalk
15. draft	drift	drip	15. driftwood
16. grass	grand	glass	16. grasshopper
17. house	hard	home	17. homesick
18. ninth	nail	name	18. fingernail
19. teeth	tool	tooth	19. toothache
20. worm	wood	wrist	20. woodpecker
21. stairs	stars	start	21. upstairs
22. wad	war	way	22. halfway
23. dress	press	bless	23. dressmaker
24. bay	tag	bag	24. handbag]

Lesson 14 | SYLLABLES

[This lesson presents syllabication and accent, following the authority of Webster's *New International Dictionary*, Second Edition, Unabridged, in these details of word analysis.]

AUDITORY IDENTIFICATION: SYLLABLES AND ACCENT

Listen to the words I am going to say. [As you say each word of more than one syllable, emphasize the syllable divisions.]

bag   rab'bit   po · ta'to

How many times did I use my voice when I said *rab'bit?* (2) when I said *po · ta'to?* (3) when I said *bag?* (1)

When you pronounce a word, each time you use your voice you say a **syllable.** How many syllables are in *bag?* Yes, one. In *rab'bit?* Yes, two. How many syllables are in *po · ta'to?* Yes, three syllables.

When a word has more than one syllable, we generally say one syllable with more force than we give to the other syllables. In *rab'bit,* which syllable do we say harder? Yes, the first syllable, *rab.* In the dictionary, the word is printed like this: **rab'bit.** [Write it on the board.] The mark after the first syllable is an **accent mark.** The accent mark tells which syllable to **accent,** or say harder.

Say *potato.* [Pause.] Which syllable did you accent? Yes, the middle syllable, *ta.* This is the way the dictionary prints **po·ta'to.** [Write it on the board.] Which syllable has the accent mark?

AUDITORY IDENTIFICATION: VOWELS

Every syllable has one or more vowels in it. What vowel do you hear in the one-syllable word, *bag?* Yes, short *a.* [Write *băg.*]

What vowels do you hear in each syllable in *rabbit?* Yes, short *a* in the first syllable [Mark ă.] and short *i* in the second syllable. [Mark ĭ.] But we scarcely hear the *i* in the second syllable *bit* because we do not accent that syllable.

What vowels do you hear in *potato?* Yes, long *o* in the first syllable [Point.], long *a* in the second syllable [Point.], and long *o* in the third syllable. [Mark the vowels in the word on the board: *pō · tā'tō.*]

Listen to this word: *ba'by.* [Write it on the board.] What is the vowel in the first syllable? Yes, long *a.* [Mark ā.] Look at the second syllable. [Point.] How does the letter *y* sound? Yes, it sounds like short *i.* [Write *bā'bў.*]

1. I am going to say some more words. Listen to the vowel sound in each syllable. [Call on a child for the answer to each question you ask.]

Listen: "bug." How many syllables in *bug?* Yes, one syllable. What vowel do you hear in *bug?* Yes, short *u.* [Write *bŭg* on the board.]

Listen again: "ex·cept'." How many syllables in *except?* [Call on a child.] Yes, two syllables in *except.* What vowels did you hear in these syllables? Yes, short *e* and short *e*. [Write ĕx·cĕpt′ on the board.]

[Continue in the same way with the remaining 12 words.

Words		Vowels		Words		Vowels
1. bug	(1)	(u)		8. in·vite′	(2)	(i, i)
2. ex·cept′	(2)	(e, e)		9. ex·cuse′	(2)	(e, u)
3. pen′ny	(2)	(e, y)		10. ra′di·o	(3)	(a, i, o)
4. pic′nic	(2)	(i, i)		11. vi·o·lin′	(3)	(i, o, i)
5. pock′et	(2)	(o, e)		12. cab′i·net	(3)	(a, i, e)
6. tab′let	(2)	(a, e)		13. key′hole	(2)	(e, o)
7. brace′let	(2)	(a, e)		14. vi′o·let	(3)	(i, o, e)]

2. [See that each child has paper and pencil. Direct the children to write the numbers 1–20 in a column at the left.]

I am going to say a number and a word. After the right number on your paper, write the *number of syllables* you heard in the word and draw a circle around that number. [Say the word clearly, emphasizing the syllable division. The words and the correct responses are given below.]

1. en·joy′ing	(3)		11. fin′ger		(2)
2. bi′cy·cle	(3)		12. pil′low		(2)
3. li′on	(2)		13. pock′et·book		(3)
4. an′i·mal	(3)		14. no′bod·y		(3)
5. fol′low·ing	(3)		15. pump′kin		(2)
6. in′stant	(2)		16. hur′ry		(2)
7. in′stant·ly	(3)		17. quar′rel		(2)
8. op′po·site	(3)		18. nine·teen′		(2)
9. li′brar·y	(3)		19. hand′ker·chief	(3)
10. fac′to·ry	(3)		20. dan′ger·ous		(3)

[Check by reading aloud the number of the word and the number of syllables in the word.]

VISUAL AND AUDITORY IDENTIFICATION

1. [List the following words, with their numbers, on the board. Do not show the syllable division as given in parentheses. Keep the list on the board for the second exercise.

After you write a word, pronounce it and pause slightly between syllables. Ask the children to pronounce it after you.]

1. telephone (tel′e·phone)
2. agree (a·gree′)
3. football (foot′ball)
4. laundry (laun′dry)
5. follow (fol′low)
6. path (path)
7. family (fam′i·ly)
8. jolly (jol′ly)
9. kept (kept)
10. instead (in·stead′)
11. unkind (un·kind′)
12. largest (larg′est)
13. monkey (mon′key)
14. basket (bas′ket)
15. hero (he′ro)
16. beginning (be·gin′ning)
17. earnest (ear′nest)
18. tomato (to·ma′to)
19. envelope (en′ve·lope)
20. strawberry (straw′ber·ry)
21. invite (in·vite′)
22. beast (beast)
23. avenue (av′e·nue)
24. leaf (leaf)
25. dangerous (dan′ger·ous)
26. grandfather (grand′fa·ther)
27. nobody (no′bod·y)
28. grocery (gro′cer·y)
29. general (gen′er·al)
30. finish (fin′ish)

2. [Direct the children to take out paper and pencil. Then ask them to draw two lines to divide their paper into three vertical columns as shown on page 72. Demonstrate from the board, showing columns and headings.

Then direct them to copy the thirty words in exercise 1 above from the board, putting each word, with its number, in the correct column.

The correct responses follow on page 72.]

one-syllable words	two-syllable words	three-syllable words
6. path	2. agree	1. telephone
9. kept	3. football	7. family
22. beast	4. laundry	16. beginning
24. leaf	5. follow	18. tomato
	8. jolly	19. envelope
	10. instead	20. strawberry
	11. unkind	23. avenue
	12. largest	25. dangerous
	13. monkey	26. grandfather
	14. basket	27. nobody
	15. hero	28. grocery
	17. earnest	29. general
	21. invite	
	30. finish	

[Direct a check of the children's responses by naming the correct words for each column. Ask the children to check the spelling of each word they wrote by comparing it closely with the word on the board.]

3. [Ask the children to write the twenty-six letters of the alphabet, using the small-letter form. Ask them to circle *a, e, i, o,* and *u.* Then ask them, "What are the letters *a, e, i, o, u* (and *y*)? What are the other letters called?"]

Lesson 15 | SUFFIXES *ED* AND *ING*: EFFECT ON FINAL CONSONANT

AUDITORY AND VISUAL

1. [Write the words in Column 1 (below) on the board. Point to and pronounce word number 1. Then call on individual children to answer the following questions about the word.

(*a*) How many syllables does this word have?

(*b*) What is the last (final) letter in the word? Is that final letter a consonant or a vowel?

(*c*) What is the vowel in the word? Say the word. (Pause.) Does the vowel have the long sound or the short sound?

Then proceed in the same way with each of the other words.

Column 1	Column 2	Column 3
1. scrub	1. scrubbed	1. scrubbing
2. shop		
3. slip		
4. step		
5. stir		
6. trap		
7. trim		
8. plan		
9. skin		
10. drag]		

2. You often use the words in this column. [Point to Column 1.] You use them when you speak and sometimes when you write. Watch how I change the word *scrub*.

[Write *scrubbed* and *scrubbing* in their respective columns.]

I added *ed* and *ing* to *scrub*. What did I do before I added those endings? Yes, I doubled the final consonant *b* in *scrub*.

Say *scrubbed*. [Pause for group response.] Does *scrubbed* have one syllable or two? [One.]

Say *scrubbing*. How many syllables in *scrubbing*? [Two.]

[Explain the technical terms and develop the rule as follows.]

The simple word *scrub* [Point to it in Column 1.] is called a base or a **root word**. A new ending added to a root is called a **suffix**. [Underline *ed* and *ing* in *scrubbed* and *scrubbing*.] *Ed* and *ing* are *suffixes*.

Do *ed* and *ing* begin with vowels or with consonants? Yes, both these suffixes begin with vowels.

Here is a rule to guide you when you add these suffixes to a root word. [Read the rule to the group. If it seems desirable, write the rule on a chart for future reference.]

When you add a suffix that begins with a vowel to a one-syllable word that has a short vowel right before the final consonant, double this final consonant of the root word before you add the suffix.

See whether you can follow this rule as you finish Columns 2 and 3. Who will write *shopped* and *shopping*? [Call on an individual child.]

[When a child has written these words in their respective columns, ask the group to check.]

Did _?_ follow the rule? Is *shop* a one-syllable word? Does *shop* end in a consonant with a short vowel before it? Did _?_ double that final consonant *p* when he (she) added *ed* and *ing* to *shop*?

[Continue with the rest of the words in the same way.]

3. Say the words in Column 2 [Point.] — the words that have the suffix *ed* added to the root words. [Point to each word and have the group respond.] Do these words have one syllable or two? [The answer is *one*.]

Now say the words in Column 3 — the words that have the suffix *ing*. [Point and pause as above.] Do these words have one syllable or two? [The answer is *two*.]

[Elsewhere on the board, write *scrubbing* and *shopping*.] See how I divide these words into syllables. [Draw lines between the syllables.]

scrub/bing   shop/ping

Where does the syllable division come? Yes, it comes *between* the double letters.

[Call on children to draw the lines for syllable division in the rest of the words in Column 3. Then develop the rule.]

When a word has had its final consonant doubled because the suffix ing *has been added, the syllable division comes between the double letters.*

4. [Write the following words on the board. Have individual children draw lines to show the syllable divisions.

1. canning	6. tripping	11. hemming
2. cutting	7. dropping	12. flitting
3. hopping	8. snapping	13. dripping
4. running	9. swimming	14. fanning
5. tipping	10. flapping	15. getting]

5. Some one-syllable words to which *ed* has been added have two syllables.

[Write the following words on the board. Have the children pronounce them. Then call on individual children to draw lines to show the syllable division in the words.

nodded	skidded	knitted	plodded
batted	fretted	chatted	spotted
flitted	strutted	budded	trotted]

Lesson 16 | **SUFFIXES *ED* AND *ING*: DROPPING FINAL *E***

AUDITORY AND VISUAL

[Write the headings *Column 1*, *Column 2*, and *Column 3* on the board. Then list the following words in Column 1.

Column 1	*Column 2*	*Column 3*
1. bake		
2. chase		
3. dance		
4. hope		
5. share		
6. slide		
7. smile		

8. smoke

9. wave

10. love

11. wipe

12. like

13. arrive

14. tumble

15. believe

16. invite

17. divide

18. measure]

1. [Have the children pronounce each word after you as you say it and point to it.]

With what letter does each of these words end? [The letter *e*.] When you said each of these words, did you hear the final *e?* No, the final *e* is **silent**.

Now see what happens when I add the suffixes *ed* and *ing* to some of these words. [Write *baked* and *baking, chased* and *chasing* under their respective headings. Draw a circle around the *ed* or *ing* in each word.] What happened to the silent *e* in *bake* and *chase* when *ed* and *ing* were added? Yes, the silent *e* was dropped. Remember this rule. [Write it on the board or on a chart.]

> *When you add a suffix that begins with a vowel to a root word that ends in silent* e, *drop the silent* e.

[Continue.] Who will come to the board and add *ed* and *ing* to word number 3? [Call on an individual child and have him write *danced* and *dancing*. After he has written the words, have the group check.] Did _?_ follow the rule? Did he (she) drop the silent *e* before adding *ed* and *ing?* [Continue in the same manner with the rest of the words in Column 1.]

2. [Take up the problem of syllabication.] Listen as I say these words from Column 2. [Repeat through word number 12, as the last six words have two syllables before the suffixes are added.] Did you hear one syllable or two syllables in each word? Yes, the suffix *ed* did not add a syllable to these words in Column 2.

Does *baking* [Point.] have one syllable or two syllables? Yes, *baking* has two syllables. Say the word and pause between the syllables. Now I will draw a line to divide the word into two syllables: (bak/ing). Where did I draw the line? Yes, just before the suffix *ing*. [Call on individuals to show the syllable division in words 2–12 in Column 3.]

3. [Words numbered 13–18 are two-syllable words ending with silent *e*. Handle these words as suggested for words 1–12. They follow the rule given on page 77 for words 1–12.]

4. [Direct the children to take out paper and pencils and write the headings *Column 1*, *Column 2*, and *Column 3*. Write the three headings on the board, and also the following words on the board. Then direct the group to copy the words with their numbers in Column 1:

1. ache	5. close	9. bounce	13. cave
2. live	6. shave	10. breathe	14. care
3. wade	7. bathe	11. change	15. wake
4. use	8. save	12. shade	16. rule

Direct the group to add *ed* and *ing* to each word, writing the other two forms in Columns 2 and 3. After the children finish, direct a check. On the board, write the three correct forms of each word, and have the children check each word they wrote on their papers.]

Lesson 17 | SUFFIXES *ED* AND *ING:*

WORDS ENDING IN Y

[Write the headings *Column 1*, *Column 2*, and *Column 3* on the board. Complete Column 1 as shown.

Column 1	Column 2	Column 3
1. dry	dried	drying
2. cry		
3. try		
4. pry		
5. spy		
6. hurry		
7. empty		
8. carry		
9. ferry		
10. reply		

Then proceed as follows.]

1. With what letter does each of these words end? [Point.] Yes, with *y*. Now look at the letter *before* the final *y* in each word. [Point to that letter in each word.] Are these letters consonants or vowels? Yes, they are consonants.

Sometimes you must add *ed* or *ing* to a word ending in *y* with a consonant before it. Watch to see how to do that. [Write *dried* in Column 2.] What did I do to the word *dry* before I added *ed* to it? Yes, I changed *y* to *i* and then added *ed*.

Now see how I add *ing*. [Write *drying* in Column 3.] Did I change anything in *dry* when I added *ing*? No, I did not.

Now watch to see how I add *ed* and *ing* to *cry*. [Write *cried* and *crying*.] Who will explain what I did?

[Let individual children volunteer to write the two forms of the remaining words in Column 1. Have each child explain what he did. Then refer the group again to Column 1. Emphasize the point that each word ends in *y*, and that the letter preceding the *y* is a consonant. Keep the three columns on the board for later checking, but cover them.]

2. [Using the same procedure, present the fact that a word ending in *y* with a vowel before it *does not* change when *ed* or *ing* is added. List the following words:

1. stay	3. pray	5. enjoy	7. employ
2. play	4. obey	6. delay	8. destroy

Since these words present no difficulty, be sure to make the contrast between them and the words in exercise 1. Review exercise 1. Leave both sets of words on the board, but cover them.]

3. [Have children take out pencil and paper. Direct them to write *Column 1*, *Column 2*, and *Column 3* across their papers. Then list on the board, one at a time, six words selected from exercise 1, with the words in exercise 2 intermingled. Have the children write the three forms of each word under the proper headings. Check the papers, either by passing about among the children and checking especially Column 2; or, have the children check their own papers by the words on the board, now uncovered.]

Lesson 18 | SUFFIXES *ED* AND *ING*: WORDS THAT DO NOT CHANGE

[Exercise 1 presents words ending with a single consonant preceded by two vowels. On the board, write the headings *Column 1*, *Column 2*, and *Column 3*. List the following words in Column 1.

1. rain	6. dream	11. bloom	16. boil
2. gain	7. lean	12. look	17. spoil
3. fail	8. clean	13. soak	18. roar
4. wait	9. treat	14. wheel	19. pour
5. chain	10. peep	15. cheer	20. shout]

1. Look closely at each word in Column 1. With what kind of letter does each word end? [Point to the final letters.] Yes, each word ends with a consonant.

How many vowels do you see before each final consonant? [Underline the two vowels in each word.] Yes, there are two vowels before each final consonant.

Watch as I add the suffixes *ed* and *ing* to *rain*. [Write *rained* and *raining* in the appropriate columns.] Did I change *rain* in any way when I added *ed* or *ing*? No, these words add *ed* or *ing* without any change. [Call on individual children to add *ed* and *ing* to the remaining root words, writing the words in the appropriate columns on the board.]

2. [A second type of word that does not change when *ed* or *ing* is added is one that ends with two or three consonants. Proceed with an exercise based on these words as suggested for exercise 1, using the words that follow:

touch	howl	spill	match
burn	land	thank	light
climb	laugh	wash	watch
coast	learn	reach	search
comb	sign	roll	patch]

3. [The following exercise is in the nature of a review. Ask the children to take out paper and pencil. Direct them to write the headings *Column 1, Column 2,* and *Column 3* across the paper. On the board, write those same column headings.]

I am going to say a word and write it in Column 1 on the board. You are to write the word in Column 1 on your paper. In Columns 2 and 3, write the word with the suffixes *ed* and *ing* added. Think carefully about each word.

[Here are the words for the teacher to dictate and for the children to write in Column 1:

1. grab	7. laugh	13. wrap	19. wade
2. bake	8. close	14. stir	20. stay
3. reach	9. trap	15. cry	21. carry
4. enjoy	10. smile	16. dance	22. empty
5. spoil	11. learn	17. play	23. clean
6. lock	12. chase	18. try	24. float]

[When the children have finished, question individual children.] Jerry, how shall I write *grabbed?* How shall I write *grabbing?* [After you have written the forms, have the children check those forms on their papers. Continue in the same way with each of the twenty-four words.]

[For use as a constant reminder and reference, prepare a manila chart to give the following information.]

Words That Do Not Change When the Suffixes ed and ing Are Added

1. Words that end in *w* or *y* preceded by a vowel; as, *snow, stay.*
2. Words that end in one consonant preceded by two vowels; as *heat, sail.*
3. Words that end in two or three consonants; as *earn, rest, watch.*

Lesson 19 | USING OTHER SUFFIXES

[In previous lessons, the suffixes *ed* and *ing* have been presented. Lesson 19 presents the following suffixes:

er	as in *baker* (one who)	*able*	as in *laughable*
y	as in *misty*	*ful*	as in *cheerful*
ly	as in *slowly*	*fully*	as in *helpfully*
er	as in *harder* (more)	*ness*	as in *kindness*
est	as in *hardest*	*less*	as in *fearless*
ment	as in *agreement*	*tion*	as in *invention*]

[Write the following on the board:

Word	+	Suffix	=	New Word
1. farm	+	er	=	
2. dust	+	*y*	=	
3. clear	+	ly	=	
4. clean	+	er	=	
5. clean	+	est	=	
6. enjoy	+	ment	=	
7. enjoy	+	able	=	
8. care	+	ful	=	
9. cheer	+	fully	=	
10. bright	+	ness	=	
11. hope	+	less	=	
12. collect	+	tion	=	

Then proceed with exercise 1, which is based on the list above.]

1. In the last several lessons, you learned about the suffixes *ed* and *ing*. Here are some other suffixes that you sometimes add to words. [Point to each suffix in the middle column on the board. Have the children pronounce each suffix as you point to it.]

Who will write the new word that you make when you add *er* to *farm*? [Call on a child to come to the board and write it.] What word did _?_ make? [Have the group pronounce *farmer*.] Did the suffix *er* add a new syllable to the word *farm*? Was the word *farm* changed in any way when the suffix *er* was added?

[Proceed in the same way with the rest of the words. Children may note that the word *collect* drops the final *t* when *tion* is added. If not, call attention to this fact as a lead into exercise 2.]

2. [Expand the idea that changes in spelling may occur when a suffix is added to some words. Proceed as follows. Demonstrate with one type of change at a time.]

Sometimes there is a change in spelling when a suffix is added to a word. Here are some words that change.

[Write the following on the board:

1. big + er = bigger
2. win + er = winner
3. hot + est = hottest]

How did the spelling of each word change when the suffix was added? Yes, the final consonant was doubled. See the double *g* in *bigger;* [Point.]   the double *n* in *winner;* [Point.]   the double *t* in *hottest.* [Point.]

Watch as I write these words:

[Write:

4. day   + ly = daily
5. happy + er = happier
6. pity   + ful = pitiful]

How did I change each word when the suffix was added? Yes, I changed the final *y* to *i.* [Point.]   Watch as I write these words:

[7. bake   + er   = bak/er
8. like   + able = lik/able
9. shade + y   = shad/y
10. gentle + ly   = gent/ly]

How did I change the spelling of these words when the suffix was added?   [Point to 7, 8, and 9.]   Yes, the silent *e* was dropped. What happened to *gentle* [Point.] when *ly* was added? Yes, *le* was dropped.

Some words that end in silent *e* do not drop the *e* when a suffix that begins with a consonant is added. Notice these words

[Write:

  11. amuse + ment = amusement
  12. hope + less = hopeless]

When *tion* is added, most words change their final letter or letters. Tell what change occurs when *tion* is added to these words.

[Write on the board:
  13. attend + tion = attention   [Final d is dropped.]
  14. correct + tion = correction   [Final t is dropped.]

Turn to your dictionary when you are not sure how to change the root word when a suffix is added.

3. [On the board, write only the underlined root words below. Ask the children to make as many new words as they can from each word by adding suffixes. When a child suggests a new word, have him write it below the underlined word, and, if there is a change in the root word, explain the change. The listed words suggest words that children might well think of.

hard	love	happy
harder	lovely	happier
hardest	loveliness	happiest
hardly	lovable	happily
hardness	lovableness	happiness
great	heavy	agree
greatly	heavier	agreed
greatness	heaviest	agreeing
greater	heavily	agreeable
greatest	heaviness	agreement

change	care	like
changed	cared	liking
changing	caring	likely
changeable	careful	likeable
changeless	carefully	likeness
changeableness	careless	likeableness
	carelessness	

AUDITORY AND VISUAL IDENTIFICATION

4. [Have the children turn to Worksheet 9.] Look at exercise 1. [Read the direction with the group.] See the 15 rows of suffixes. I will say a word for each row. Listen for the suffix in the word. Find the suffix in the row and circle it. Begin: "Row 1 — taking." [Continue with the words that follow. Correct responses are underlined.]

1. taking	_ing_	est	ed	er
2. lovable	less	y	est	_able_
3. baker	_er_	est	ing	ful
4. politest	able	er	_est_	y
5. snowy	er	_y_	ing	est
6. thankful	ing	y	_ful_	tion
7. safely	er	_ly_	est	ness
8. restless	ly	est	ing	_less_
9. swiftly	_ly_	y	ful	tion
10. longer	est	ness	ing	_er_
11. protection	_tion_	est	er	ing
12. darkness	_ness_	er	ful	ly
13. enjoyment	fully	less	tion	_ment_
14. thoughtfully	est	ful	_fully_	able
15. nodded	tion	_ed_	er	ly

[When the exercise is completed, direct a check.] I
will say a number and a word; then I will say the suffix
that should be circled: "Row 1 — taking. There should be a
circle around *ing*." [Continue with each row.]

5. Look at exercise 2 on Worksheet 9.

[Read the direction with the children. If desirable, use
words 1 and 2 as samples, writing them on the board and having
a child circle the suffix in each word.

Here are the words with the suffix in each underlined:

1. work<u>ing</u>	7. care<u>ful</u>	13. move<u>ment</u>	19. act<u>ion</u>
2. safe<u>ly</u>	8. fear<u>less</u>	14. danc<u>ing</u>	20. cloud<u>y</u>
3. excite<u>ment</u>	9. enjoy<u>able</u>	15. crowd<u>ed</u>	21. fin<u>est</u>
4. swift<u>ly</u>	10. kind<u>ness</u>	16. lov<u>able</u>	22. help<u>ful</u>
5. long<u>er</u>	11. grow<u>er</u>	17. thought<u>fully</u>	23. care<u>less</u>
6. thank<u>fully</u>	12. gay<u>est</u>	18. elect<u>ion</u>	24. cheer<u>y</u>

When children finish, direct a check of their work.

Do not have Worksheet 9 detached from the booklet, as
Worksheet 10 is on the reverse side.]

Lesson **20**

HOW SOME PREFIXES
AFFECT WORD MEANING

You know that a suffix is a new ending added to a
word. Today's lesson is about a syllable that is placed
in *front* of a word. Such a syllable is a **prefix.**

1. [Present the prefix *re*.] I am going to write some words on the board. Then I shall place the prefix *re* before each word. It will give the word a different meaning.

[Write the following words. Underline each prefix.

read	fill	write
reread	refill	rewrite]

Do you see how the prefix *re* changes the meaning of each word? It makes *read* mean "read again." You can *read* a poem and then you can *reread* it. What does *refill* mean? What does *rewrite* mean?

[Write the following words on the board. Ask individual children to come to the board and make a new word by prefixing *re* to a word; then to give a sentence that uses the new word.

tell	build	load	enter
teach	join	plant	open]

2. [Present the prefix *un*. Proceed as with prefix *re* above. Write the following words on the board:

happy	clean	fold	load
unhappy	unclean	unfold	unload]

What did the prefix *un* do to each word? Yes, *un* gave each word the opposite meaning. *Un* means *not;* therefore *unhappy* means *not happy*.

[Write the following words on the board. Have individual children write *un* before a word; then give a sentence using the new word.

able	healthy	even	kind
dress	cover	equal	steady]

[For each of the exercises on page 90, use the listed words in the same manner as such words were used in exercises 1 and 2. If necessary, pronounce the root words for the group.]

3. Present the prefix *im* (meaning *not*).

[Examples for teaching:

perfect	polite	possible
imperfect	impolite	impossible]

[Bring out the fact that *im* often gives a word the opposite meaning.]

[For pupils to build:

pure	movable	passable
proper	patient	modest]

4. Present the prefix *dis* (meaning *not*).

[Examples for teaching:

like	honest	obey
dislike	dishonest	disobey]

[For pupils to build:

order	please	agree
place	contented	believe]

5. Present the prefix *in* (meaning *not*).

[Examples for teaching:

correct	attention	direct
incorrect	inattention	indirect]

[For pupils to build:

expensive	definite	action
accurate	dependent	complete]

6. [Have the children turn to Worksheet 10, which is on the back of Worksheet 9. Direct the children's attention to exercise 1. Read the direction with them. Use words 1 and 2 as samples to illustrate what the children are to do, if it seems desirable.]

[After the children have completed the exercise, direct a check, saying, "Number 1, *displease*, — a circle around *dis*." Here are the words with the correct response underlined.

1. displease	6. revisit	11. unfriendly
2. imperfect	7. undress	12. impolite
3. unhappy	8. improper	13. dissatisfy
4. retell	9. displace	14. reorder
5. inexpensive	10. inexact	15. infrequent]

7. [Direct the children's attention to exercise 2 on Worksheet 10. Read the direction with them.] I will say a row number and a word. Listen for the prefix in the word. Find that prefix in row 1 and draw a circle around it.

[The words to be dictated are listed below. Repeat the number of the row as well as the word. The correct response is the underlined prefix.

1. recall	**re**	im	in
2. displace	im	**dis**	re
3. impolite	un	re	**im**
4. incorrect	un	**in**	im
5. undress	im	in	**un**
6. repack	**re**	im	in
7. unhappy	**un**	im	in
8. displease	re	in	**dis**

Direct a check of the exercise by repeating the word and naming the prefix.]

Lesson 21 | REVIEW

[This lesson reviews initial and final consonants; initial and final consonant blends; prefixes and suffixes; visual recall of words. It is based on Worksheet 11.

Examine the worksheet before taking up each exercise with the children. There are three exercises, and it is suggested that these exercises be taken up at separate periods.

Before taking up exercise 1, recall to the children's minds such terms as *consonant, beginning* and *final consonant, blend,* and *beginning* and *final blend;* also, recall that there are two- and three-letter blends. Perhaps it will be advisable to write several words on the board to demonstrate each of these various concepts. Call attention to rows 21–25 on the back of the worksheet.

Have the children turn to Worksheet 11. Read the directions for exercise 1 with the group.

Use rows 1, 2, and 3 as samples, directing the children closely until they know just what they are to do.]

EXERCISE 1. BEGINNING OR FINAL LETTERS OR BLENDS

[The words to be dictated are given on page 93 opposite. Say the row number and the word. The right responses in each row are underlined. Direct a check after each five rows.]

(Sample)	1. zip	q	**z**	a	o	y	th	**p**
(Sample)	2. trim	**tr**	br	t	th	**m**	n	r
(Sample)	3. stir	f	b	sh	**st**	p	ch	**r**
	4. bloom	**bl**	n	p	b	**m**	l	w
	5. swift	sh	ch	**sw**	b	p	c	**ft**

——————————————————————————Check and discuss

	6. log	**l**	cr	dr	b	f	**g**	k
	7. match	th	**m**	fr	w	**tch**	sh	t
	8. form	p	i	**f**	**rm**	r	j	rn
	9. camel	**c**	t	h	**l**	p	s	q
	10. dress	**dr**	br	p	b	h	**s**	tr

——————————————————————————Check and discuss

	11. youth	**y**	st	sp	**th**	tch	v	wh
	12. shed	sw	**sh**	ch	p	**d**	g	sm
	13. proof	gr	**pr**	dr	nt	**f**	t	pl
	14. streak	thr	sh	**str**	spr	b	h	**k**
	15. golf	m	**g**	p	b	**lf**	th	lt

——————————————————————————Check and discuss

	16. seven	**s**	**n**	z	t	rt	c	x
	17. roast	d	l	**r**	nt	**st**	k	t
	18. whiz	**wh**	b	**z**	m	o	v	w
	19. sleep	st	**sl**	cl	**p**	sn	fl	gl
	20. tax	p	**t**	b	n	**x**	z	f

——————————————————————————Check and discuss

	21. club	**cl**	**b**	nd	ld	d	rd	rl
	22. hold	**h**	th	**ld**	st	b	lp	mp
	23. scorch	p	**sc**	r	nt	**rch**	pt	ct
	24. varnish	b	**v**	t	p	**sh**	rth	nch
	25. north	s	t	**n**	nch	ch	rch	**rth**

Check and discuss]

EXERCISE 2. PREFIXES AND SUFFIXES

[Direct the group to exercise 2 on the back of Worksheet 11. Read the first direction (for rows 1–5) with them. Be sure that they know what to do. The words to be spoken are given below. The correct responses are underlined.

Dictate	*Correct Responses*			
1. unclean	in	im	dis	<u>un</u>
2. reread	dis	un	<u>re</u>	in
3. dishonest	re	in	im	<u>dis</u>
4. impatient	<u>im</u>	re	dis	in
5. inattentive	im	<u>in</u>	re	un

Check the children's responses by reading the word and the correct prefix to be circled in each row.]

[Read the direction (for rows 6–12) with the children. The words to be spoken and the correct responses follow.

6. dictation	<u>tion</u>	est	er	ing
7. fearless	ly	<u>less</u>	er	ment
8. kindness	ment	less	<u>ness</u>	tion
9. helpful	ly	y	<u>ful</u>	fully
10. hardest	er	<u>est</u>	ful	ed
11. baker	<u>er</u>	est	ful	ment
12. slowly	y	<u>ly</u>	ful	fully

Check the children's responses by reading the word for each row and then giving the correct suffix.]

EXERCISE 3. WORDS

Look at exercise 3 on the back of Worksheet 11. [Read the direction with the group.] I am going to write a word with the number of the row before it. Then I will erase the word. Find that word in the row and circle it.

[The words to be written on the board, with the row number for each word, are given here.

1. prepare	3. grocery	5. flowing	7. throat
2. drawer	4. crown	6. telegram	8. sweater

Direct a check of the children's work. On the board, rewrite the row number with the correct word beside it. Have the children compare with their own responses.]

Lesson **22** | **IDENTIFYING LETTERS WITHIN WORDS**

[This lesson presents directions and materials for Worksheet 12. Preceding lessons have dealt with letters and sounds at the beginnings or endings of words. On Worksheet 12, the pupils are called upon to identify single letters and blends within words.]

VISUAL IDENTIFICATION AND VISUAL MEMORY: CONSONANTS

[Exercise 1 of Worksheet 12 calls for visual identification and visual memory of single consonants within words. Direct the children to turn to Worksheet 12. Read the direction for exercise 1 with them. Then proceed as suggested here.]

In exercise 1, see the six rows of letters. I will tell you what you are to do. Listen closely.

I will write a row number and a word on the board. Look at the word closely. Notice every letter that is in the word. You will have to remember all the letters, not just the beginning and ending letters. When I erase the word, look at row 1 on your worksheet. Find a consonant in row 1 that you saw near the middle of the word that I wrote. Circle that letter.

[The words to be written on the board and the consonants to be circled are given here:

      1. airplane l   3. wooden d   5. unable b

      2. visit   s   4. answer w   6. waited t]

[Direct a check by writing each word on the board and underlining the consonant as above.]

AUDITORY IDENTIFICATION: VOWELS

[Exercise 2 of the worksheet calls for identification of the vowel sounds within spoken words. If it seems necessary to recall the correct markings to indicate the short and long vowel sounds, display the chart that was suggested in Lesson 10.]

Look at exercise 2 on your worksheet.   [Read the direction with the group.]   I will say a number, and then I will say a word of two syllables. Listen closely to hear the vowel sound in each syllable. On the line beside the number that I say, write the two vowels that you heard in the word. Put the right mark over each vowel to show whether you heard the short or the long sound of that vowel.

[Demonstrate from the board what is to be done by trying out several samples with the children. Here are some words that might be used for that purpose: *willow* ĭ ō; *begin* ē ĭ; *upset* ŭ ĕ.

The words to be dictated, with the correct response after each word, are given on page 97. Direct a check of the children's responses after each five words.

1. lightning	ī ĭ		11. highway	ī ā
2. payday	ā ā		12. sparrow	ă ō
3. ticket	ĭ ĕ		13. follow	ŏ ō
4. music	ū ĭ		14. blanket	ă ĕ
5. window	ĭ ō		15. bedtime	ĕ ī
6. insect	ĭ ĕ		16. polish	ŏ ĭ
7. napkin	ă ĭ		17. cutting	ŭ ĭ
8. sunset	ŭ ĕ		18. Sunday	ŭ ā
9. subject	ŭ ĕ		19. shadow	ă ō
10. daylight	ā ī		20. contest	ŏ ĕ]

AUDITORY AND VISUAL IDENTIFICATION: BLENDS

[Exercise 3 of Worksheet 12 calls for auditory identification of consonant blends *within* words. Read the direction with the group. Direct as follows.]

Look at exercise 3 on Worksheet 12. You have learned that, when two or three letters together make a single sound, the sound is called a *blend*. Look again at the rows of blends on your worksheet. Notice that some of them are made up of two letters and some of three letters.

I will say a row number and a word. Listen closely to the word so that you can hear the blend in the *middle* of the word. Then look at the row with that number and draw a circle around the blend that you heard in the middle of the word that I said.

[If it seems desirable, demonstrate the procedure with several words, such as *kitchen* (*tch*) and *wonder* (*nd*). The words to be dictated, with the correct responses, are given here.

1. marching (rch) 3. catcher (tch) 5. teacher (ch)
2. golden (ld) 4. dishes (sh) 6. luncheon (nch)]

[Exercise 4 of Worksheet 12 presents a paragraph that the children are to read, study, and then write from dictation. Direct as follows.]

Look at exercise 4 on Worksheet 12. Read the direction. Then read the paragraph. [Pause for the reading. Then proceed as follows.] In what kind of story would you find a paragraph like the one you have just read? Yes, in a fairy tale. Now read the paragraph again, this time very slowly. Look closely at each word. [Pause.]

Which words have double letters in them? [*shook, horrible, too, grabbed, all, sudden*] [Write the words on the board as the children name them.]

Which words have blends? [*swung, forth, earth, shook, each, step, started, faster, reached, grabbed, with, cried, stop*] [Write the words.]

Now turn your worksheet over. I will dictate the story. Write each sentence or part of a sentence after I say it. Spell each word right.

The giant was coming. His arms swung back and forth. The earth shook at each step. His big ugly face was horrible. John started to run faster and faster, but it was too late. The giant reached out and grabbed him with his huge hands. Then all of a sudden a voice cried, "Stop." The giant quickly put him down.

[After the children have finished writing, direct them to check their work. Spell the words yourself and call on children to spell them.]

Lesson 23 | SUFFIXES: SPECIAL USES

[This lesson presents suffixes that are added to words for these purposes: to form the plurals of singular nouns and to make descriptive words (adjectives) express degrees of comparison. The lesson is based on Worksheet 13. The children should have a pencil and Worksheet 13 at hand.]

MAKING NAMES MEAN MORE THAN ONE

1. Look at your worksheet. [Read the direction for exercise 1 with the group.] Read the names in part *A* of exercise 1.

[Call on a child to read the ten words aloud as the other children read silently. Here are the words in part *A* on the worksheet:

| coin | girl | house | cake | airplane |
| doll | nest | shell | book | button] |

Do you remember what a word that names a person, place, or thing is called? [A *noun*.] Does each noun in part *A* name one or more than one? [One.] A noun that names only one is called a **singular noun.**

How can you make each singular noun in part *A* mean more than one? [Call on a child.] Yes, by adding

s to it. A noun that names more than one is a **plural noun.**
Now look again at part *A* on your worksheet. Write the
plural form of each singular noun. [When the children have
finished, write the plural forms on the board and have them
check their responses.]

2. Look at part *B* on your worksheet. [Have a child
read the words aloud.] Does each noun name one or more
than one? Yes, each noun in part *B* is a singular noun.

[Here are the words in part *B*:

ax	dish	bus	lunch	dress	patch
fox	wish	gas	branch	glass	watch]

These singular nouns end in *x, sh, s, nch, ss,* and *tch.*
To form the plurals of nouns having endings like these,
you have to add *es.* [On the board write *match — matches;
class — classes; bench — benches; tax — taxes.* Call attention to the ending of each singular form and then to the
suffix *es* that forms the plural.]

Now take up part *B* on your worksheet. Write the
plural form of each singular noun. [When the children
have finished, write the plural form of each noun in part
B on the board. Have the children check their responses.]

3. [Direct the group to read silently the words in part *C* on
their worksheets. Then ask one child to read the words aloud.
Here is the list:

lady	penny	family	journey	birthday
key	country	grocery	community	chimney]

With what letter does each of these nouns end? Yes,
with the letter *y.* In which nouns do you see a vowel before
y? [*key, journey, birthday, chimney*] A noun that ends
in *y* with a vowel before it forms its plural by adding only *s.*

Which words in *C* end in *y* with a consonant before the *y?* [Have children point to and name the words.] When a noun ends in *y* with a consonant before it, change the *y* to *i* and add *es* to form the plural.

In part *C* of exercise 1 on your worksheet, write the plural form of each word on the line after the word. [When the children finish, write the plural forms on the board and have the children check what they wrote.]

MAKING WORDS EXPRESS COMPARISON

[On the board, write the following sentences:

    1. Joe is *tall.*

    2. Jim is tall*er* than Joe.

    3. Bob is the tall*est* boy in the class.

Then proceed as suggested here.]

Tall is a describing word. [Point to *tall.*] Read the sentences on the board and notice how *tall* is changed. [Pause.]

In sentence 1, *tall* describes Joe. In sentence 2, *taller* [Point.] compares Jim's height with Joe's. In sentence 3, *tallest* [Point.] compares Bob's height with the height of all the boys. What suffixes were added to *tall* to make it show such comparison? Yes, *er* and *est*. These suffixes are added to many describing words to make them show comparison. When these suffixes were added to *tall*, was *tall* changed in any other way? No, it was not.

[Write the following sentences on the board:

    4. Here is a *funny* picture.

    5. I have a funn*ier* picture.

    6. Jill drew the funn*iest* picture of all.]

What happened to *funny* when *er* and *est* were added to it? [Point.] Yes, the final *y* in *funny* was changed to *i*.

[Write the following sentences on the board:

7. We had a *gay* time.
8. This dress is gay*er* than that one.
9. The trees are gay*est* in fall.]

With what letter does the describing word *gay* end? [*y*] What kind of letter comes before the *y* in *gay*? [A vowel.] Did *gay* change when *er* and *est* were added? [No.] Here is a rule to remember. [Write on board.]

When er *and* est *are added to a word that ends in* y *with a consonant before it, change* y *to* i *and add* er *or* est. *When* y *has a vowel before it, just add* er *or* est *without changing* y.

Now look at exercise 2 on the back of Worksheet 13. [Read the direction with the group.]

Read sentence 1 to yourself. [1. Mary arrived _?_ than John.] Who can think what form of *soon* belongs in the sentence? [Call on a child.] Yes, *sooner* belongs in the sentence. Write *sooner* on the line.

Read sentence 2 to yourself. [2. John's second arithmetic paper is _?_ than the first.] What form of *neat* belongs in the sentence? [If everyone responds correctly, direct the group to write *neater* on the blank line. Then direct the group to complete the ten sentences.]

[At the close, direct a check. Ask individual children to come to the board and write the word they wrote in a given sentence, proceeding with one sentence at a time. After the group approve (or correct) each word that is written, have them check the word that they themselves wrote to see whether they spelled it correctly. The correct responses are as follows:

1. sooner	3. neatest	5. easiest	7. gayest	9. happier
2. neater	4. longer	6. sunnier	8. drier	10. busiest]

Lesson **24** | WORDBUILDING

[This is a lesson in wordbuilding by the use of the prefixes and suffixes presented in Lessons 19 and 20. It is advised that the teacher glance through those lessons to recall the background for this lesson.]

1. In earlier lessons you learned that you can make longer words from a word root by adding one or more prefixes or suffixes to it. [Question as follows to review the terms.]

    a. Who can give an example of a word with a prefix? [Children may give such examples as *tie — untie; write — rewrite; place — displace.*]

    b. Who can give an example of a word with a suffix? [Children may give such examples as *care — careful — careless; kind — kindly — kindness.*]

[Continue such questioning until children reveal that they recall the earlier lessons and understand the terms *root word, prefix,* and *suffix.*]

2. I will write a word on the board. Then I will make new words from it by using prefixes and suffixes. Think what each word is and what it means. [Write the following and then question as indicated.

agree

disagree

agreeable

disagreeable

agreement]

 a. What is the root word? [Point to *agree.*] Who will give a sentence using *agree?* [Call on several individual children.]

 b. What is this word? [Point to *disagree.*] Who will come to the board and underline the prefix? Who can use the word in a sentence? [Call on individual children.]

 c. [Present the other three words in the same way.]

3. [Continue the same procedure with the following words. Where a change in spelling occurs as a suffix is added, as in *excuse,* call attention to such changes.

break	kind	care
break*able*	kind*ly*	care*ful*
*un*break*able*	kind*ness*	care*less*
	*un*kind	care*fully*
pass	place	excuse
pass*able*	*re*place	excus*able*
*im*pass*able*	*dis*place	*in*excus*able*]

4. [This exercise is based on exercise 1 of Worksheet 14. Exercise 1 continues on the back of the sheet.]

Look at exercise 1 on Worksheet 14. Notice the five groups of words. The first word in each group is a root word.

The others are words that were built by adding prefixes or suffixes. [Read the direction for exercise 1 with the group.]

I will say the words in each group. I will give a sentence that shows the meaning and use of each word. After each sentence, I will say the word again. Then look at the words that follow the root word. Draw a circle around any prefix or suffix that you find.

[Here are listed the words and sentences that the teacher is to read aloud:

1. possible   It is possible that we may have rain.
   impossible   Then it will be impossible to have the picnic.
   possibly   Father may possibly take us in his car.
2. natural   The accident was a natural result of his carelessness.
   unnatural   It was unnatural for Allen to be idle.
   naturally   Father's arrival was naturally a surprise.
   unnaturally   The weather was unnaturally warm in January.
3. like   The boys worked like beavers.
   likely   It is likely that their team will win.
   unlikely   It is unlikely that we can reach home by noon.
4. usual   We followed our usual plan.
   unusual   Nothing unusual happened that day.
   usually   Jack is usually on time.
   unusually   The day was unusually warm.
5. enjoy   Did you enjoy the circus?
   enjoyment   The clown added to our enjoyment.
   enjoyable   We had an enjoyable time at Tim's party.
   unenjoyable   Bad weather made our trip unenjoyable.

At the completion of the exercise, direct a check of the children's work. Have five children write the five word lists on the board and have them place the circles properly.]

5. [Take up exercise 2 of Worksheet 14. Read the directions with the group. Be sure that all have suitable books in which to search for words. Let the children work for about eight or ten minutes. Then have the individuals read the words they have listed, and, in each word, name the root and the prefix or suffix.]

Lesson **25**

WORDS BUILT FROM
THE SAME ROOT

[See that children have Worksheet 15 before them. Note that the exercise continues on the back of the sheet. Read the direction with the group. Then proceed as follows.]

1. kick
   kicked
   kicking

   a. Look at the words in group 1 on your worksheet. Pronounce them after me. [Dictate the words clearly.]

   b. How are these words alike? [They have the same root word.]

   c. How does adding the suffix *ed* change the meaning? [It makes the word tell that something has happened.]

   d. Divide *kicking* into syllables. [kick/ing]

       e. Write the three words on your work-sheet.

2. note   *a.* Pronounce the words in group 2 after
  notes   me. [Dictate them.]
       b. How are they alike? [Same root word.]
       c. What does *note* mean? [*Note* means
        "a short letter."] How does this mean-
        ing change when *s* is added? [*Notes*
        means more than one.]
       d. Write the two words on your work-sheet.

3. bench   *a.* Pronounce the words in group 3 after
  benches   me. [Dictate.]
       b. What is the difference in the meaning
        of the two words? Which one means
        more than one? [*Benches.*]
       c. How is the plural of a name (noun)
        ending in *ch* formed? [Add *es.*]
       d. Write the words on your worksheet.

4. body   *a.* Pronounce the words in group 4 after
  bodies   me. [Dictate.]
       b. How is the plural of a name (noun)
        ending in *y* preceded by a consonant
        formed? [Change the *y* to *i* and add
        es.]
       c. Write both words on your worksheet.

5. lĭve   *a.* Listen as I pronounce the words in
  lĭves (līves) group 5. [Dictate.]
  lĭved   *b.* Spell *lively* and *lĭving* in syllables after
  lĭvely   me: [līve/ly, lĭv/ing]. Do you notice
  lĭving   that the final *e* was dropped before

adding the *ing* in *living?* Why was it dropped? [A final silent *e* is dropped when a suffix that begins with a vowel is added.]

c. Why wasn't the *e* in *lively* dropped? [Because the suffix *ly* does not begin with a vowel.]

d. Give a sentence using *līves*. Give a sentence using *lĭves*.

e. Write the five words on your worksheet.

6. move
moving
movement

a. Look at group 6 at the top of the right column on your worksheet. Listen as I pronounce these words. [Dictate.]

b. Look at *moving*. Why was the final *e* in *move* dropped before adding the suffix *ing?* [Because the suffix *ing* begins with a vowel.]

c. Look at *movement*. Why wasn't the silent *e* dropped before adding the suffix *ment?* [Because *ment* does not begin with a vowel.]

d. Write the words on your worksheet.

7. float
floating

a. Listen to the words in group 7. [Dictate.]

b. With what blend do they begin? [*fl*]

c. What sound does the *oa* have? [ō]

d. What is the suffix in *floating?* [*ing*]

e. Write the two words on your worksheet.

8. laugh
laughed
laughing

a. Listen to the words in group 8. [Dictate.]

b. How are they alike? [Have the same root.]

c. What is the sound of *gh* in *laugh?* [f]
Spell *laugh* with me: l-a-u-g-h.

d. Write the three words on your worksheet.

9. lead
   leader
   leading

a. Listen to the words in group 9. [Dictate.]

b. How are they alike? [Have the same root.]

c. What sound does the *ea* have? [ē]

d. What are the suffixes of the last two words? [*er* and *ing*]

e. Write the words on your worksheet.

10. learn
    learned
    learning

a. Listen to the words in group 10. [Dictate.]

b. Spell the part that is alike in the three words.

c. What are the suffixes of the last two words? [*ed* and *ing*]

d. Write the words on your worksheet.

11. protect (pro·tect)
    protected (pro·tect·ed)
    protection (pro·tec·tion)

a. Listen as I say the words in group 11. [Dictate.]

b. I will say each word again and pause between syllables. Spell each syllable when I pause.

c. How does the suffix *tion* sound? [*shŭn*]

d. Look at each word carefully. Spell the words in syllables to yourself.

e. Write the three words on your worksheet.

12. happy — unhappy
like — unlike
welcome — unwelcome

a. What prefix has been added to the root word in each pair? [*un*]
b. Give sentences using *unhappy*, *unlike*, and *unwelcome*.
c. Write the six words.

13. farm — farmer
build — builder
help — helper
sing — singer
bank — banker

a. Listen as I say the words in group 13. [Dictate.]
b. Often the name of a person who does something is formed by adding the suffix *er* to the word that tells what he does. Tell what the second word in each pair means.
c. Write the ten words on your worksheet.

14. machine (ma·chine)
machines (ma·chines)

a. Listen as I say the words in group 14. [Dictate.]
b. What blend do you hear in the middle of each word? The *ch* sounds like *sh*. How does the vowel *i* sound? Yes, like long ē.
c. Study the words carefully. They are not spelled just as they sound.
d. Write the two words.

[Direct the children to check by comparing each word they copied with the printed word from which they copied.]

Lesson **26** | **UNDERSTANDING THE DICTIONARY**

LOCATING WORDS

1. [Direct the children to take out their dictionaries. Have them leaf through them briefly, noting that the listed words (entries) are printed in heavy black type; also, that they are listed in alphabetical order. Then proceed as follows.]

A good "word detective" knows how a dictionary is arranged. Hold your closed dictionary with its back resting on your desk. With your thumbs, divide the book into three even parts. Now open it where your left thumb is placed. With what letter do the words on the pages begin? [Probably *e* or *f*, depending on how accurately the child has divided the book.] Now open it where your right thumb is placed. What pages do you see? [Probably pages showing *m*, *q*, or *r*.] Now you have one steer for locating a word. [On the board, write the following.]

First Third	Middle Third	Last Third
a, b, c, d, e, f,	g, h, i, j, k, l,	q, r, s, t, u, v,
	m, n, o, p,	w, x, y, z

[Have each child place a paper clip in his dictionary on the last page of the *f* words and another on the last page of the *p* or *q* words. Then proceed as follows with a list that you have previously written on the board. Use the list given below. Call on individual children.]

2. To which part of the dictionary would you turn if you wished to find *dangerous?* Yes, to the first part. To which part would you turn to find *program?* Yes, the middle part.

[Continue with the rest of the following list in the same manner.

1. dangerous (first)	5. bowl (first)	9. weave (last)
2. juice (middle)	6. coast (first)	10. neither (middle)
3. sly (last)	7. ladder (middle)	11. waste (last)
4. usual (last)	8. muster (middle)	12. worms (last)]

ALPHABETICAL ORDER

3. [Read the following paragraph aloud:

The boys on Pleasant Street were playing "Detective." Uncle Tom, the best fisherman in town, had told them they could go fishing with him if they could find him before it started to rain. The only clue they had was a sheet of note paper that Uncle Tom had left on the breakfast table at his house. Five words were on the sheet: *at, fat, digging, creek, worms.*

The boys were puzzled. "Let's put the words in alphabetical order and see if they give us a clue," said George. The boys went to work with pencils. Soon they had their clue.]

[Write the five words in the order shown above.] Can you get a clue from these words? [Point.] Look at the first letter in each word. Name the words in alphabetical order and I will write them on the board. [Write the words in sentence form as the children name them: *At creek digging fat worms.*]

4. [Ask the children to take out paper and pencils. Have the following lists on the board:

List 1	List 2	List 3
engine	fruit	slab
airplane	flag	slope
weather	fortune	sly
rudder	feel	sled
pilot	fire	slip
hangar	fable	slush]

Look at the words in List 1. Do they begin with different letters? Yes. To write them in alphabetical order, you need to look at the first letter. [Underline the first letters.] Write the title "List 1" on your paper. Under it write these six words in alphabetical order. [When the children finish, have them check as you name the words in alphabetical order.]

Now look at List 2. Do the words begin with the same letter or with different letters? [Same.] Then you need to look at the second letter in these words in order to write them in alphabetical order. [Underline the second letter in each word. Proceed as with List 1.]

[Then discuss List 3, in which the third letter in the words must be considered. Have the children write the words in alphabetical order and then check.

With children in grades 5 or 6, provide a fourth list to give children practice in alphabetizing by the fourth letter. Use these words: *blaze, black, blame, blade, blast, blanket*.]

USING GUIDE WORDS

5. At the top of each page in the dictionary are two words that are called *guide words*. [Illustrate by displaying a dictionary page.] The one at the left is the same as the first word on the page. The one at the right is the same as the last word on the page. All the words that come alphabetically between the guide words can be found on that page. [On the board, place the following copy of the guide words on two facing pages.]

Page		
banana	120	bar

Page		
barb	121	burn

[Question as follows.] Would you find *bank* on page 120 or on page 121? [120] On what page would you find *bandit?* [120] *barber?* [121] *barley?* [121]

6. [Have the following chart with its list of words and the column headings on the board:

WORD	PAGE IN DICTION- ARY	LEFT-HAND GUIDE WORD	RIGHT-HAND GUIDE WORD
1. quart	_____	_____	_____
2. saucer	_____	_____	_____
3. bouquet	_____	_____	_____
4. harness	_____	_____	_____
5. sirup	_____	_____	_____
6. kennel	_____	_____	_____
7. dapple	_____	_____	_____
8. heave	_____	_____	_____]

Take out paper and a pencil. Arrange your papers as shown on the board. Find each word in the dictionary. After the word, write the correct information under each column heading.

[When the pupils finish, direct a check. Ask pupils to name the correct responses for each word and write them after the word on the board. Then have pupils check their own papers.]

Lesson 27 | GETTING HELP FROM THE DICTIONARY

[Syllabication and diacritical markings in this lesson are based on Webster's *New International Dictionary*, Second Edition, Unabridged.]

PRONUNCIATION AND MEANING

1. Bill read this sentence in a book he was reading: [Write the sentence on the board.]

The explorers found the bones of a mammoth.

Mammoth was a new word to Bill. He wanted to know how to pronounce it and what it meant. In his dictionary, this is what he read: [Write on the board.]

> **mam′moth** (măm′ŭth) A huge elephant no longer in existence.

There was also a picture of a mammoth that showed him what this creature had looked like. [Point to the word **mam′moth** on the board. Then question as follows.]

a. How many syllables does *mammoth* have? [Point.] Where does the syllable division come? [Between the two *m*'s in the middle of the word.]

b. After which syllable do you see the mark (') that is called an *accent mark?* [Point.] Yes, the first. The accent mark tells which syllable to stress, or say hardest.

c. Look at the word in parentheses. [Point.] See how the vowel *a* in the first syllable is marked. Does it have the long sound (ā) or the short sound (ă)? [The short sound.] Say that sound.

Look at the second syllable as given in parentheses. [Point.] The *o* in this syllable is to be pronounced like short ŭ. Say that sound.

Now pronounce the whole word. [Point to each syllable as the children pronounce it.]

d. In an earlier lesson, you learned that this mark (⁻) over a vowel gives the vowel the long sound. The mark is called a **macron.** This mark (˘) over a vowel gives the vowel the short sound. It is called a **breve.** Such marks are called **diacritical marks.**

Turn to the front of your dictionary and find the key to pronunciation. [Help the children find it.] You can see that there are other diacritical marks, some for vowels and some for consonants. When you find a word in the dictionary and do not know what a certain diacritical mark means, turn to this key for help. (As children examine the key, call attention to a few of the more common markings such as ä, o͝o, o͞o and the like.)

2. Find each of the following words in your dictionary. Pronounce each word to yourself. Study its syllables, the accent marks, and the diacritical mark or marks. Look at its meaning. We shall work out one together on the board. [Present from the board as follows.]

Word	Syllables	Pronunciation	Meaning
1. dogie	do·gie	(dō'gǐ)	A motherless calf in a cattle herd.
2. bruin			
3. igloo			
4. galleon			
5. palanquin			

Arrange your papers in columns like those on the board and write the correct heading for each. Do the other words by yourself. Use the key to pronunciation in your dictionary when necessary.

SPELLING

3. Your dictionary is a help in learning how to spell a word that you wish to write and in checking your written work. Read this story that Kathy wrote. [Have the following story written on the board in advance, and point to it now.] Each word that Kathy misspelled is in parentheses. As I point to each of those words, use your dictionary to find its correct spelling. [Give the pupils time to find each word; then call on individuals to erase a misspelled word and write the correctly-spelled word in its place.]

I have been reading some of the tall (tails) of Paul Bunyan. He was a (mitey) (loger). He could (straiten) out a river, scoop out a (canion), turn a (mountan) under, and tinker with the (wether).

4. In the word *center*, *c* sounds like *s*. In *came*, *c* sounds like *k*. In each sentence I write, the first letter in one word is missing. Tell whether it should be a *c*, an *s*, or a *k*. Use your dictionary if you are not sure.

[Write the sentences on the board one at a time.

1. We all __ept very quiet.
2. Not even a __ough was heard.
3. Put the tea __ettle on the fire.
4. How shall we __ettle the argument?
5. When do we __elebrate Washington's birthday?
6. We could not be __ertain of the weather.
7. Did you forget your __erchief?
8. I did not have a __ingle penny.]

5. I will write a word twice. One is spelled right and one is wrong. Use your dictionary to find out which is spelled right.

[Write the two forms of each word on the board. Say the word. After children have checked with the dictionary, have one child come forward and cross out the incorrect word.

(neither	(leather	(board
(niether	(lether	(baord
(message	(travel	(piece
(mesage	(travle	(peice
(effort	(begger	(wepon
(efort	(beggar	(weapon
(library	(suprise	(grateful
(libary	(surprise	(gratefull
(appear	(baloon	(damige
(apear	(balloon	(damage
(dence	(cooky	(engine
(dense	(cookey	(enjine]

6. [If the pupils use a spelling text that offers rules or procedures for studying a word, or if you have a manila chart presenting rules that you have devised, you will not need the following rules. If there are no other rules in use, write the following rules on a manila chart and have them ready for use. Display the chart and explain as follows.]

Sometimes you have to learn to spell a new and difficult word that you have looked up in the dictionary. Here are some suggestions on how to study a word.

How to Study Spelling
1. Say the word to yourself.
2. Look at the word carefully. Notice its syllables. See how each syllable is spelled.
3. Close your eyes and spell it in syllables.
4. Open your eyes and see if you spelled it correctly.
5. Write the word from memory.
6. Check what you have written.
7. Cover the word and write it again.
8. Write it correctly in your own alphabetized spelling notebook.

Use the rules in studying each of these words. [Have the words on the board.]

1. surprise 3. rough 5. arithmetic 7. fault 9. sleigh

2. library 4. barrel 6. February 8. juice 10. suppose

[Erase or cover the words. Then dictate them and have the children write them. Afterward, have the children check their spelling by referring to the dictionary.]

Lesson 28 | SYLLABLE DIVISION

OPEN SYLLABLES

1. [Before taking up this exercise, write the following lists of words on the board:

List 1	List 2
secret	sunset
parade	almost
giant	banjo
music	napkin
motor	enjoy

Direct the children to find each word in List 1 in the dictionary and note the syllable division. Then call on individual children to tell how the word is divided.

Mark each word as follows as the children tell the syllable division:

se/cret   pa/rade   gi/ant   mu/sic   mo/tor]

How many syllables has each of the words in List 1? [Two.]

Does the first syllable in each word end with a vowel or a consonant? [With a vowel.]

A syllable ending with a vowel is called an **open syllable.**

CLOSED SYLLABLES

2. [Take up the syllabication of the words in List 2 in the same manner, having children consult their dictionaries for the syllable division. Mark the correct division as children report their findings, as follows:

sun/set   al/most   ban/jo   nap/kin   en/joy]

How many syllables does each word in List 2 have? [Two.] Does the first syllable in each word end with a vowel or a consonant? [With a consonant.] A syllable that ends with a consonant is called a **closed syllable**.

Look at the second syllable of each word in List 2. In which word is the second syllable an open syllable? [banjo]

[For further practice, have the children (*a*) find the following words in their dictionaries; (*b*) note the syllable division in each; (*c*) tell how many syllables each word has; (*d*) tell whether each syllable is open or closed.

extra   zebra   tepee   solo

depend   circus   beneath   attic]

DIVIDING WORDS HAVING DOUBLE CONSONANTS

3. [List the following words on the board.

bubble   barrel   mitten   sudden   hammer]

What do you see in the middle of each of these words? [Point.] Yes, a double consonant. Say each word after me. [Repeat the five words.] How many syllables has each word? Yes, two.

[As before, have children consult their dictionaries to find the syllable division for each word. Call on individuals to draw lines in the words to show the division. Then help the children to formulate this generalization: When a two-syllable word has a double consonant in the middle, the syllable division comes between the two consonants.]

WORDS WITH TWO DIFFERENT CONSONANTS IN THE MIDDLE

4. [Have the following words on the board.]

  wonder except danger turkey practice

What do you see in the middle of each of these words? [Point to the middle of each word.] Yes, two different consonants.

[Proceed as in the previous exercise. Have the children find each word in their dictionaries, and then draw a line to mark the syllable division. There can be no definite rule for words of this type, for some similar words do not divide between the consonants. To bring out this fact, put the following list on the board:

  bother cracker pocket husky father]

THREE-SYLLABLE WORDS

5. [Write the following words on the board:

tomato	December	umbrella
yesterday	vacation	nobody
radio	telephone	together
already	seventy	accident

Follow these steps:

a. Say each word and have children tell how many syllables they heard.

b. Have them find each word in the dictionary and then mark it to show its syllable division.

c. Have them analyze each word to tell which syllables in it are open and which are closed.]

SYLLABLE DIVISION IN WRITTEN WORK

6. When you write a paragraph or a story, you sometimes find that you need to divide a word at the end of a line. When you do, you should divide it at the end of a syllable. Here are some points to remember:

(1) Do not divide a one-syllable word, such as *thought* or *wrong* or *sleeve*. If it will not fit at the end of the line, write the whole word on the next line.

(2) Divide a word of two or more syllables at the *end* of a syllable. If you need help as to the syllable division, consult your dictionary.

(3) Place a hyphen at the end of the syllable at which you divide a word.

(4) Do not divide a short word such as *able, any, into*, and *only*.

In the next exercise, remember these rules.

WRITTEN PRACTICE

7. [See that children have paper and pencils ready.]

On Worksheet 12 for Lesson 22, you had a dictation exercise. Turn to that worksheet and study the paragraph again — the paragraph about a giant. [Pause to give the group the necessary time. If Worksheet 12 has been torn from the book, write the paragraph on the board, as follows:

The giant was coming. His arms swung back and forth. The earth shook at each step. His big ugly face was horrible. John started to run faster and faster, but it was too late. The giant reached out and grabbed him with his huge hands. Then all of a sudden a voice cried, "Stop." The giant quickly put him down.]

Now I will dictate the paragraph. [When you dictate, read a complete sentence and have the group listen to it. Then dictate by phrases within the sentence.] If you need to divide a word at the end of a line, remember what you have learned in this lesson about syllables within words and about dividing at the ends of syllables.

[At the close of the dictation, ask each child who found it necessary to divide a word to go to the board and show how he divided it. Ask the rest of the group to check by the dictionary to see whether the division is correct. Then have the children check one another's papers for correct spelling, punctuation, capitalization, and the like.]

Lesson **29** | **MORE ABOUT SYLLABLES**

The words that you need to learn to spell come from three sources:

(1) There are the words in your regular spelling list or spelling text.

(2) There are other words that you wish to use when you write personal letters, or write a lesson, a story, or a report in school. Some boys and girls keep such words in their own alphabetized notebook.

(3) There are new words that you learn and use in social studies, science, or health units. It is important to learn to spell these words. Some of them are long. To study long words, it is helpful to divide them into syllables and to follow the steps for the study of a word as suggested on your spelling study chart. [See Lesson 27.]

This lesson will help you to master new words that you want to write or need to write.

1. [Ask the pupils to refer to Worksheet 16. On the board write the headings *Column A* and *Column B*.]

Look at the words in Column A on your worksheet. They are words you might need to use in a Health and Safety Unit. I will say the first word and use it in a sentence. Think how to divide the word into syllables, and which syllable is accented. Consult your dictionary if necessary. Divide the word on your worksheet into syllables, like this: *po/lice/man*. [Write on board.] Then put in the accent mark. Is everyone ready? [Dictate.]

Column A

1. ac'/ci/dent   Was anyone hurt in the <u>accident</u>?

[Write *accident* on the board but do not divide it into syllables. Then have a child mark the word to show how he marked it on his worksheet.]

2. dan'/ger/ous   The slippery roads are <u>dangerous</u>.

[Write *dangerous* (not divided) while the pupils are marking it.] Show us how you marked it, John.

[Continue as suggested for 1 and 2 on page 125.

3. of'/fi/cer	At the corner stood a traffic <u>officer</u>.
4. o/be'/di/ence	We believe in strict <u>obedience</u> to traffic rules.
5. pre/ven'/tion	Practice fire <u>prevention</u> in the home.
6. hand'/ker/chief	When you sneeze, cover your nose with your <u>handkerchief</u>.
7. clean'/li/ness	<u>Cleanliness</u> is important to health.
8. um/brel'/la	Carry the <u>umbrella</u> so that you can see where you are going.
9. tem'/per/a/ture	The correct room <u>temperature</u> is 68 degrees.
10. care'/less/ness	Many accidents are due to <u>carelessness</u>.]

Column B

2. Column B consists of words from a unit on Our Neighborhood. Look at Column B on your worksheet.

[Follow the procedure suggested for Column A.

1. de/liv'/er	The newsboy will <u>deliver</u> the papers.
2. gro'/cer/y	The <u>grocery</u> supplies much of our food.
3. fam'/i/ly	Each <u>family</u> is proud of our neighborhood.
4. res'/i/dents	The <u>residents</u> belong to a community club.
5. a/part'/ment	Our family lives in an <u>apartment</u>.
6. fac'/to/ry	The <u>factory</u> employs many workers.
7. beau'/ti/ful	We have a <u>beautiful</u> park.
8. li'/brar'/y	We find good books in our school <u>library</u>.
9. neigh'/bor/hood	This is not a business <u>neighborhood</u>.
10. com/mun'/i/ty	It is a residence <u>community</u>.]

3. [This exercise is planned for five groups of pupils with five in each group. If there are more or fewer than twenty-five children in your class, adapt the group arrangements as needed. Also, adapt the number of words in each list to the number of children in each group.

Each group should have at least one dictionary; if all the children have dictionaries, each child may use his own. Have the following five lists of words on the board.

Give each group a number, and explain that each group is to work with the list of words that bears the number of the group; that is, Group 1 will handle the words in List 1.]

When I say "ready," the first pupil in each group is to find in the dictionary the first word in his group list. When he finds the word, he is to go to the board, draw lines that divide it into syllables, and place the accent mark. Then the next person in that group will do the same for the second word; and so on. The first group to finish their list with all words correct is the winner.

List 1	*List 2*	*List 3*
1. whatever	1. afterwards	1. passenger
2. addition	2. forgetting	2. wandering
3. grasshopper	3. understand	3. invention
4. violet	4. mosquitoes	4. happily
5. specially	5. easiest	5. unwelcome

List 4	*List 5*
1. yesterday	1. telegram
2. enliven	2. obeying
3. geography	3. reminded
4. equally	4. listening
5. receiving	5. entertain

[The correct syllable and accent markings are given here for the teacher's use in checking the children's work.

List 1	List 2	List 3
what/ev′/er	aft′/er/wards	pas′/sen/ger
ad/di′/tion	for/get′/ting	wan′/der/ing
grass′/hop/per	un/der/stand′	in/ven′/tion
vi′/o/let	mos/qui′/toes	hap′/pi/ly
spe′/cial/ly	eas′/i/est	un/wel′/come

List 4	List 5
yes′/ter/day	tel′/e/gram
en/liv′/en	o/bey′/ing
ge/og′/ra/phy	re/mind′/ed
e′/qual/ly	lis′/ten/ing
re/ceiv′/ing	en/ter/tain′]

Lesson **30** | **ANALYZING SPELLING WORDS**

[Direct the children to have paper and pencils ready.]

1. [Write *whenever* on the board and pronounce it. Then read the sentence that follows it (below) and pronounce the word again. Ask questions *a* and *b* (page 129) and give direction *c*.

whenever   We will go whenever you are ready.]

a. What two words make up this word? [*when* and *ever.*]

b. What do we call a word that is made up of two smaller words? [a compound word]

c. Spell the word with me, pausing after the first half of the word: w-h-e-n/e-v-e-r. Now write the word on your papers.

2. [Write *wandering* on the board, pronounce it, read the sentence, and say the word again.

> wandering   The little lost boy was wandering in the woods.]

a. How many syllables do you hear in *wandering?* [three]

b. What is a syllable? [A part of a word in which you hear or say a vowel sound.]

c. What part of *wandering* is the root word? [*wander*] What is the suffix? [*ing*]

d. Spell the word in syllables with me. [Pause after each syllable.] w-a-n/d-e-r/i-n-g. Write the word on your papers.

3. [Write *trimming* on the board, pronounce it, read the sentence, and pronounce the word again.

> trimming   The children were trimming the Christmas tree.]

a. How many syllables are there in *trimming?* [two]

b. Where do you divide a word that doubles the final consonant when *ing* is added? [between the double consonants]

c. With what blend does *trimming* begin? [*tr*]

d. What sound does the *i* have in both syllables? [short *i*] *e.* Spell the word in syllables with me: t-r-i-m/m-i-n-g. Write the word on your papers.

4. [Proceed in the same way with this exercise and the next.

scratched   The cat scratched the baby.]

a. What three-letter blend begins *scratched?* [*scr*]

b. What blend of three letters do you hear in the middle of the word? [*tch*]

c. Why is the suffix *ed* added to an action word like *scratch?* [to show that the action happened in the past]

d. Spell the word with me: s-c-r-a-t-c-h-e-d. Write the word on your papers.

5. [sincerely   We were sincerely glad to hear of Mary's success.]

a. With what consonant does *sincerely* begin? [*s*]

b. How many syllables do you hear in *sincerely?* [three]

c. What sound does the *i* in the first syllable have? [short *i*]

d. How is the middle syllable spelled? [c-e-r-e]

e. What is the suffix? [*ly*] The *y* has the sound of short *i*.

f. Spell the word in syllables with me: s-i-n/-c-e-r-e/l-y. Write the word on your papers.

[Erase the words from the board.] Now you will take a test on the five words. Turn your paper over and write the words on the other side. [Dictate the words. After they have been written, have the children check their spelling of the words as you spell each one.]